The
How and Why
of
Cookery

The How and Why of of Cookery

Third and fully revised Edition

N. M. Haselgrove, B.Sc. and K. A. Scallon, B.Sc.

Hart-Davis Educational

Granada Publishing Limited
Hart-Davis Educational Limited
First published in Great Britain 1963 by Arco Publications

Reprinted 1964 (twice), 1966, 1967, 1970
Second edition 1974 by Hart-Davis, MacGibbon Limited
Third edition (non-net) published 1976 by
Hart-Davis Educational Limited
Frogmore, St Albans, Hertfordshire
Third edition reprinted 1977, 1978

ISBN 0 247 12727 2

Printed in Great Britain by
Fletcher & Son Ltd, Norwich

Contents

The How and Why of Cookery

This book is intended for use by candidates at Ordinary Level in the General Certificate of Education. It will help them to enjoy the theory of the work by making them curious about

1. The HOW of the subject, that is, general rules for preparation of food and methods of cooking, planning of meals and of kitchens;
2. The WHY, that is, practical reasons for these rules and scientific reasons for the methods given.

This book will give an interesting and instructive background to the study of Food and Nutrition at any level, and also will be useful to those pupils not sitting for examinations.

It is not a recipe book.

The authors have had considerable experience in different types of school in teaching the subject; one of them has recently been an examiner in Food and Nutrition for several University examining boards and has served for some years as Chief Examiner in this subject for one of them.

THE HOW AND
WHY OF

Cookery

ONE

Food

*What it is and why we need it – What nutrients are – The
action of heat on nutrients – How the body deals with
nutrients – Proteins, fats, carbohydrates, mineral substances,
vitamins and water.*

A food is any substance, solid or liquid, which after being swallowed can be digested and absorbed into the blood stream, and then used by the body in a variety of ways to maintain life.

Why we eat food

1. For body building. Food is needed to provide materials for building all body tissues while we are growing, and for repairing all body tissues which are constantly wearing out.

2. For energy giving. Food can be 'burnt' in the body to provide the energy for maintaining the body temperature, and for the working of all the body organs even while the body is at rest, e.g. heart-beat, lung action. It is also needed for all physical activities either at work or at play.

3. For protection against ill-health. Food helps to maintain health by regulating the processes of living and growing, by controlling the production of energy, and by preventing certain 'deficiency diseases'.

Nutrients

A nutrient is a food constituent which has a definite function to perform in our bodies. The nutrients necessary for healthy growth are:

> Proteins
> Carbohydrates
> Fats
> Mineral Substances
> Vitamins
> Water

Each has its own part to play in the production of a healthy body. A food may contain more than one nutrient, e.g. cheese contains proteins, fat, water, mineral substances and vitamins.

The chief uses of the nutrients are:

1. For body building: proteins; mineral substances; water.
2. For energy giving: carbohydrates; fats; proteins, if more are taken than are needed for body building.
3. For regulating body processes: mineral substances; vitamins; water.

For the nutrients to be usable for any of these purposes, they must be in a form in which they can be carried in the blood stream to any part of the body. Therefore the following processes affecting food must take place.

1. *Digestion.* This process takes place in the digestive tract, in which food is broken down physically by movements of the intestines, and chemically into simpler substances by action of the digestive juices.

2. *Absorption* is the process by which the digested food is passed through the walls of the digestive tract into the blood stream.

3. *Metabolism* is the name given to the complex chemical processes which food substances undergo when they are either built up into body tissues, or are broken down further for the production of heat and energy. This latter process is known as 'burning' (combustion) of food in the body.

Anabolism is the name given to the building up process.

Katabolism is the name given to the breaking down process.

The energy value of food

All foods when 'burnt', either in the laboratory or in our bodies, produce heat and energy. This energy is measured in units called kilocalories (usually written as Calories). A Calorie is the amount of heat needed to raise the temperature of 1,000 grams of water by 1 degree Celsius (Centigrade).

1 gram of carbohydrate 'burnt' in the body produces 4 Calories.

1 gram of fat produces 9 Calories.

1 gram of protein produces 4 Calories.

From the composition of food we can calculate its calorific value (i.e. the number of Calories it will produce), e.g. 25 g of Cheddar cheese contains approximately:

7 grams of protein giving 28 Calories,

10 grams of fat giving 90 Calories,

therefore the total calorific value is 118 Calories per 25 g.

Why the body needs energy from food
1. For basal metabolism, i.e. all the processes of living.
2. To maintain normal body temperature.
3. For all physical activities.

How much energy is required from food
The amount required by an individual depends on age, sex, size and state of health, and also on the amount of physical activity undertaken. A schoolgirl about sixteen years old needs about 2,500 Calories per day. A boy of the same age needs about 3,500 Calories, and a girl of fourteen who is still growing rapidly, about 2,800 Calories. A male manual worker needs about 4,000 Calories, but a sedentary worker needs only about 2,600 Calories each day.

Proteins

Proteins are one of the nutrients, and are composed of carbon, hydrogen, oxygen, nitrogen and sometimes sulphur and phosphorus. The important element is the nitrogen, as this is required for all protoplasm, and proteins are the only nutrient containing nitrogen.

Proteins are built up of simpler substances known as amino acids. There are over twenty amino acids, but of these ten must be provided by the food, as the body cannot produce them itself. Proteins can be:

(a) *Animal proteins.* These are of high biological value and contain the essential amino acids in about the same proportion in which they are found in human protein. The main animal proteins are milk, cheese, eggs, meat, fish.

(b) *Vegetable proteins.* Known also as incomplete proteins, these are of lower biological value. They contain fewer essential amino acids but those missing from one protein can be supplied by another; so the diet should contain a variety of vegetable proteins which the body can turn economically into human proteins. Vegetable proteins are found in foods such as nuts, cereals and pulses.

The How and Why of Cookery

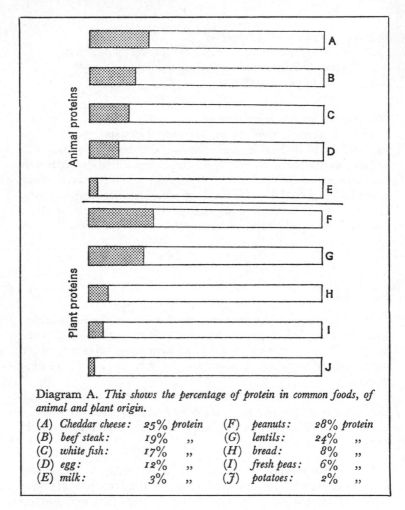

Diagram A. *This shows the percentage of protein in common foods, of animal and plant origin.*

(A)	*Cheddar cheese:*	*25% protein*	(F)	*peanuts:*	*28% protein*
(B)	*beef steak:*	*19%* ,,	(G)	*lentils:*	*24%* ,,
(C)	*white fish:*	*17%* ,,	(H)	*bread:*	*8%* ,,
(D)	*egg:*	*12%* ,,	(I)	*fresh peas:*	*6%* ,,
(E)	*milk:*	*3%* ,,	(J)	*potatoes:*	*2%* ,,

Why we need proteins
1. To provide materials for growth.
2. To repair worn out or injured tissues.
3. To provide material for building blood, enzymes, hormones.
4. To provide heat and energy.

Lack of sufficient proteins in the diet can lead to Protein Calorie Malnutrition (PCM). PCM deficiency diseases are common in poor countries, particularly where rice is the staple diet, since rice contains little protein. Thus a person whose daily requirement of Calories is provided largely by rice may suffer from PCM, resulting in lack of resistance to other diseases and premature ageing. Severe cases of PCM in young children may lead to deficiency diseases such as kwashiorkor and marasmus; if these are not treated appropriately the child is unlikely to survive.

How the body deals with proteins

Protein digestion begins in the stomach where the pepsin in the gastric juice breaks down the proteins into intermediate substances known as peptones. It is continued in the small intestine where tripsin, an enzyme from the pancreatic juice, breaks down these peptones to amino acids.

Absorption of these amino acids takes place through the walls of the small intestine into the blood capillaries, and they are then carried in the blood to the tissues.

Metabolism. The amino acids are then variously combined to form cell proteins, hormones, antibodies and other substances. Some amino acids are carried to the liver where the nitrogen is removed and the rest is 'burnt' to provide heat and energy. The main function of the proteins is to build and to repair the body tissues, and to regulate the complex body processes by making hormones, enzymes, antibodies and catalysts. The production of heat and energy is a secondary function, since these can be obtained much more economically from carbohydrates and fats.

How cooking affects proteins

1. Coagulation or setting by heat, e.g. hardening of egg white; formation of a skin on boiled milk; hardening of meat fibres.

2. This is usually followed by shrinkage, e.g. overcooked scrambled eggs, meat or cheese.

The protein value of food is not affected by normal cooking temperatures but it can be damaged by excess heat.

Carbohydrates

Carbohydrates are nutrients composed of carbon, hydrogen and oxygen, the two latter elements being in the same proportion as in water. Carbohydrates can be classed into three groups.

1. *The simple sugars, or monosaccharides.* Glucose is found in fruit and in plant juices, and is always present in human blood as it is produced during the digestion of carbohydrates; fructose is similar to glucose and is found in fruit and in honey.

2. *The double sugars, or disaccharides.* Sucrose is found in the sugar cane and in sugar beet, and in all the commercial forms of sugar produced from these. Lactose is the sugar found in milk, and maltose the sugar in malt. These three sugars are similar in composition. On prolonged cooking with acid, as in jam making, some sucrose is 'inverted', i.e. turned to glucose and fructose (invert sugar).

3. *The complex sugars, or polysaccharides.* Starch is present in the form of grains in many plant-foods, e.g. cereals, pulses, potatoes, unripe fruit. Dextrin, a slightly sweet substance, is formed by the action of dry heat on starch. Cellulose or roughage is the hard and indigestible part of plants which stimulates the movements of the digestive tract.

Why we need carbohydrate foods

1. To provide heat and energy for the work of the body.
2. To provide a store of energy for future use. Most carbohydrates can be turned into body fat and stored as such.
3. To provide roughage to stimulate the digestive tract.
4. To enable the body to 'burn' fats completely.

How the body deals with carbohydrates

Digestion of cooked starch begins in the mouth, where it is changed to maltose by the ptyalin in the saliva; uncooked starch is unaffected by ptyalin. The sugars and the maltose formed from the starch are acted on in the small intestine by amylase, an enzyme from the pancreatic juice, and by maltase, lactase and invertase in the intestinal juice to form simple sugars, e.g. glucose.

Absorption of this glucose takes place through the walls of the small intestine into the blood stream.

Metabolism takes place in the muscles and in the liver where the glucose is turned to glycogen and stored for future use. If too much glucose is absorbed, it is turned to fat and stored in the tissues. When required, glucose is 'burnt' in the muscles to provide body energy, with the production of carbon dioxide and water. A small amount of glucose is always present in the blood, 0·1 per cent.

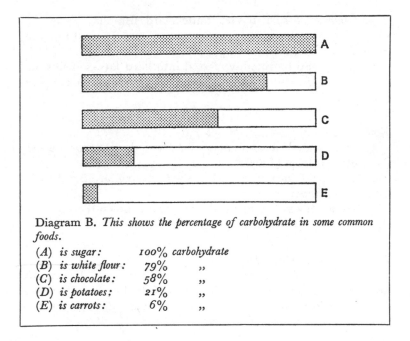

Diagram B. *This shows the percentage of carbohydrate in some common foods.*

(A) is sugar: 100% carbohydrate
(B) is white flour: 79%   „
(C) is chocolate: 58%   „
(D) is potatoes: 21%   „
(E) is carrots: 6%   „

How cooking affects the carbohydrates

Sugar melts on being heated, and turns straw colour. If heating is continued it forms a dark brown caramel, turns black to charcoal (which damages its nutritional value) and finally burns away.

Starch granules swell and burst when heated. With moist heat the starch is gelatinized and will thicken the liquid. With dry heat the starch is turned to dextrin, e.g. toast and the outside of a loaf of bread. Overheating will burn the starch granules, damaging the structure and lessening the food value.

Cellulose is softened by moist heat, but is not made digestible. It is, however, made easier to swallow, e.g. in cooked fruit and vegetables.

Fats

Fats are nutrients composed of carbon, hydrogen and oxygen, but they differ from carbohydrates in that they contain a lower proportion of oxygen. A fat molecule consists of three fatty acid units combined with one unit of glycerol. Fats can be:

(a) *Animal fats* such as suet, butter, lard, fish-oils.

(b) *Vegetable fats* such as olive, corn, and ground-nut oils, peanut butter and most margarine.

Fats may also be roughly classed into hard fats, soft fats and oils, according to their physical state at normal room temperatures.

Why we need fats

1. To provide heat and energy for the body. Fats form a very concentrated form of fuel.

2. To provide a store of fuel in the body, e.g. around the vital organs and under the skin.

3. To provide satisfying meals, as fat slows down the process of digestion and the food is longer in the digestive tract.

How the body deals with fats

Digestion. This takes place in the small intestine. The melted fats are emulsified by the alkaline salts of the bile from the liver. An enzyme in the pancreatic juice, called lipase, then breaks them down into fatty acids and glycerol.

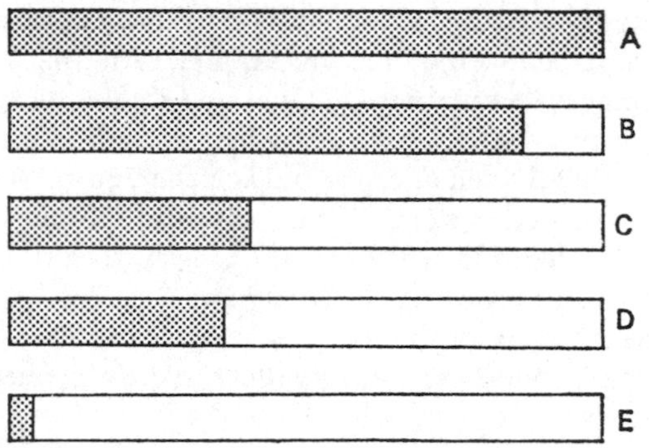

Diagram C. *This shows the percentage of fat in some common foods.*

(A) *is lard and olive oil:*   *100% fat*
(B) *is butter and margarine:*   *85% „*
(C) *is ham:*   *40% „*
(D) *is Cheddar cheese:*   *35% „*
(E) *is milk:*   *4% „*

Absorption. These products are then absorbed through the intestinal walls into the lymphatic system and thence into the blood stream.

Metabolism. The body builds up its own fats from the absorbed food fats, but most of these are 'burnt' in the tissues with the production of carbon dioxide and water, releasing heat and energy.

How cooking affects fats

Solid fats melt when heated. Some fats are liquid at ordinary room temperature, e.g. oils. Some fats have much lower melting points than others. If heating is continued, fats eventually decompose into fatty acids and glycerol, and this latter substance is further broken down to acrolein, which gives the characteristic bitter taste to overheated fat. At this stage the nutritional value is damaged.

Vitamins

Vitamins are substances present in various foods in very minute quantities, which are essential for growth and for maintaining health. The chief vitamins are:

Vitamin A or axerophthol, which helps growth, prevents infection and aids good sight.

Vitamin B_1 or aneurin (known also as thiamine), which helps growth, assists in the processes by which the body obtains energy from food, and keeps the nervous system healthy.

Vitamin B_2 or riboflavin, which helps growth, helps the body to obtain energy from food, and keeps the skin healthy.

Vitamin B_3 or nicotinic acid, which helps growth, helps in the production of energy from food and keeps the nervous system healthy.

Vitamin C or ascorbic acid, which helps growth, helps in the formation of the red blood cells, and aids the healing of wounds and broken bones.

Vitamin D or calciferol, which helps growth, builds firm bones and teeth and prevents the disease rickets in children.

The chief sources of these vitamins are:

Vitamin A: fish liver oils, animal liver, dairy foods. Green and yellow vegetables and fruits contain carotene which is converted to vitamin A on absorption into the blood stream.

This vitamin is added to margarine.

Vitamins of the B Complex: wholemeal cereals, yeast and yeast extracts, lean meat, milk, cheese, eggs and leafy vegetables. Vitamins B_1 and B_3 are added to white flour by millers.

Vitamin C: most fruits, especially citrus, and green vegetables, salads and potatoes.

Vitamin D: fish liver oils, dairy foods; it is also added during the production of margarine. This vitamin can be made from a substance present in the skin by the action of sunlight.

Why we need vitamins

If vitamins are not present in sufficient quantities in food, children fail to grow properly and lack vitality. If vitamins are lacking in adult diets, symptoms of sub-normal health develop, e.g. loss of appetite, lack of energy, depression and headaches, etc.

A serious lack of any one vitamin may lead to a deficiency disease, though these are now rare in developed countries.

> Lack of vitamin B_1 causes beri-beri.
> Lack of vitamin B_3 causes pellagra.
> Lack of vitamin C causes scurvy.
> Lack of vitamin D causes rickets.

How the body deals with vitamins

Vitamins require no digestion. The water-soluble vitamins B and C are absorbed both in the stomach and the small intestines. They perform their regulating and protective work where required and any excess is excreted in the urine. The fat-soluble vitamins A and D are absorbed in the small intestines, and any excess is stored in the liver. Vitamins of B complex and C cannot be stored in the body.

How to ensure a good supply of vitamins

1. Eat as great a variety of foods as possible, e.g. dairy foods for vitamins A, B_2 and D; fresh fruit and vegetables for vitamins A and C; meat and bread for vitamins B_1 and B_3.

2. Eat some foods raw, e.g. fruits and salads.

3. Cook foods with care to retain full vitamin content.

4. Give supplementary vitamin foods, e.g. cod liver oil, to babies, infants, expectant mothers.

How cooking affects the vitamins

Vitamin A and carotene are insoluble in water, so are not lost when foods are soaked or boiled. At temperatures normally used in cooking, they are not destroyed.

Vitamins of B complex are soluble in water and those from meat and vegetables will be retained if cooking water is used for soup or gravy, etc. They are not destroyed at the temperature of boiling water unless the water is alkaline (as it would be on the addition of sodium bicarbonate). They are destroyed by the high temperature reached in baking, frying and tinning.

Vitamin C is the vitamin most easily affected by cooking. It is soluble in water and easily lost during the soaking or boiling of vegetables. It is destroyed by plant enzymes released by bruising or grating vegetables, or by starting to cook vegetables by placing them in cold water. It is destroyed by long cooking, by using alkaline water, by keeping foods warm for long periods and by long storage of fruit and vegetables.

To preserve vitamin C during cooking:

Do not soak foods in water.
Prepare immediately before cooking.
Cook in a covered pan.
Use as little cooking water as possible.
Cook for as short a time as possible.
Avoid the use of bicarbonate of soda.
Strain and serve at once.
Use the cooking water for gravy or soup.

Vitamin D is not soluble in water, so it is not easily lost during cooking. It is not destroyed at normal cooking temperatures. It can be stored in the liver.

Mineral Substances

Mineral substances in food are those elements other than carbon, hydrogen, oxygen and nitrogen, which are necessary to the body and which must be supplied by food. There are altogether nineteen different inorganic mineral substances in the body and their total weight is about one twentieth of the total body weight. Some are present in large quantities and others in very small amounts.

Why we need minerals

1. To build strong bones and teeth. For this calcium, magnesium and phosphorus are required.

2. To help make the body cells, such as muscle, blood and nerve-cells. For this iron, sulphur and phosphorus are needed.

3. To keep all body fluids at the correct degree of acidity or alkalinity. For this sodium, potassium and chlorine are needed.

CHIEF MINERAL SUBSTANCES	WHY THEY ARE NEEDED	WHERE FOUND
Calcium	To build strong bones and teeth	Milk Cheese Egg Yolk
	To help blood to clot on wounds and cuts	Green vegetables Nuts
	To help working of muscles	Fish Added to flour
Iron	To make haemoglobin in the blood	Liver Meat Egg Yolk Pulses Dried fruit Added to flour
Iodine	To regulate the thyroid gland	Fish Drinking water Iodized salt
Sodium	To regulate composition of body fluids	Salt and all salted foods
Potassium	To regulate the working of the body cells	Fruit and vegetables
Fluorine	To strengthen teeth	Drinking water

How the body deals with mineral substances

All mineral substances when in soluble form are absorbed through the walls of the small intestine and carried by the blood stream to wherever they are needed. Iron is stored in the liver. Excess sodium is excreted by the sweat glands and the kidneys.

How to ensure that the body is supplied with essential minerals

1. Some minerals are needed in very small amounts and are present in so many foods that it is unlikely that there will be any

shortage in the normal diet. Some are needed in larger amounts, e.g. calcium and iron, or are present in fewer foods, e.g. iodine. These must be considered specially, and dairy foods, meat, vegetables, fruit and fish should be included in the diet.

2. Many mineral salts are soluble in water. Avoid soaking food and do not discard the cooking water. Serve vegetables raw when possible.

3. Some calcium and iron is not available to the body when combined with oxalic acid and phytic acid, so spinach, rhubarb and cereals must not be relied upon as the main source of these elements, as they contain these acids.

How cooking affects mineral substances

Calcium and iron are probably made more readily available to the body by cooking, and boiling in water containing these substances causes precipitation of the mineral salts on to the food.

Sodium and potassium may be lost in the cooking water but extra sodium is usually taken as salt with meals.

Water

Why we need water

1. For building the body tissues. About three-quarters of the body by weight is water.

2. For all the complex chemical changes which take place in the body.

3. As the cleansing agent and for the removal of waste substances by the sweat glands and kidneys.

4. As a solvent for all digested foods and to form the fluid part of the blood which carries these to all tissues.

5. As chief constituent of all body fluids.

How much water do we need to drink?

The body must be kept in a state of 'water balance', i.e. we must replace the water lost by:

(*a*) The kidneys as urine.

(*b*) The skin as sweat.

(*c*) The lungs as water vapour.

This water is replaced by:

(*a*) Water we make when fats and carbohydrates are 'burnt' in the tissues.

(*b*) Water in so-called solid foods.

(*c*) Water in the fluids we drink.

The average we need to drink is about $1\frac{1}{2}$ litres per day.

How the body deals with water

About one fifth of the water drunk is absorbed through the stomach walls and the rest through the small intestine walls. This enters the blood vessels and is taken to all parts of the body. Any excess is excreted by the kidneys and the skin. Some of the water present in foods is absorbed through the walls of the large intestine.

TWO

Digestion and Absorption of Food
The alimentary canal – How the food constituents are digested and absorbed.

Digestion is the process by which the food we eat is changed into simpler substances so that they can be absorbed into the blood stream and used by the body to maintain life.

This process takes place in the alimentary canal, which reaches from the mouth to the anus. By the time food reaches the anus most of the useful components have been absorbed through the walls of the canal. The substances which change the food or 'break it down' are called digestive enzymes.

The alimentary canal consists of the following parts – mouth, oesophagus, stomach, small intestine, large intestine (or colon), rectum and anus.

The food is moved through the canal by a rippling movement of the muscles in the canal walls. This movement is known as peristalsis or peristaltic action. Sphincter muscles at the lower end of the stomach (the pyloric valve) and at the anus play important parts in this process.

The food components needing digestion are:

Proteins which must be broken down into amino acids,
Fats which must be broken down into fatty acids and glycerol,
Carbohydrates which must be broken down into the simplest form of sugar – i.e. glucose.

Minerals, vitamins and water can be used by the body without being changed by digestion.

Changes take place in different parts of the canal:

In the mouth
Food is chewed into small parts by the teeth and mixed with saliva from the salivary glands. Saliva contains an enzyme amylase (ptyalin) which changes cooked starch into a form of sugar. Saliva makes the food alkaline.

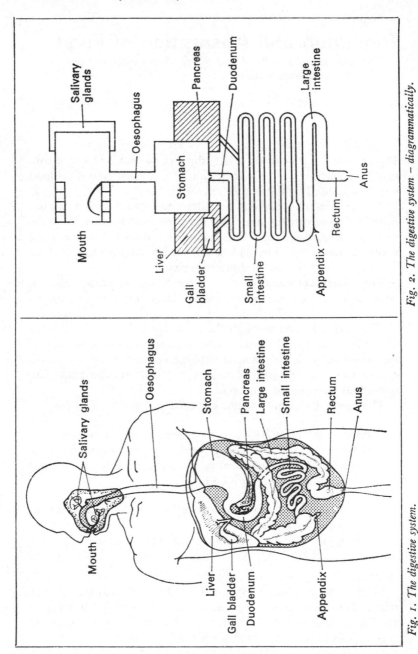

Fig. 1. The digestive system.

Fig. 2. The digestive system – diagrammatically.

In the oesophagus
No digestion takes place – it is merely a passage to the stomach.

In the stomach
Food is churned by the action of the muscles. Gastric juice comes from the stomach walls. It contains the enzyme pepsin (which begins the digestion of protein) and hydrochloric acid which acidifies the food.

In the small intestine
The first 25 cm or so of this is called the duodenum. The food is by now semi-liquid. It is acted on by three juices:

1. The pancreatic juice (from the pancreas). This contains three enzymes:
   Tripsin which breaks down proteins into amino acids.
   Lipase which breaks down fats into fatty acids and glycerol.
   Amylase which breaks down starch into maltose.
2. The bile (made by the liver and stored in the gall bladder). This emulsifies fats and makes the food alkaline.
3. The intestinal juice (from the walls of the small intestine). This contains four enzymes:
   Erepsin which acts on the proteins.
   Maltase, lactase and invertase which all act on the carbo-
       hydrates to produce glucose – the simplest form of sugar.

Digestion is now almost complete and the products can be absorbed by the walls of the small intestine, through which they pass into the blood stream and the lymph. The intestinal walls have small projections known as villi which greatly increase the surface through which absorption can take place.

In the large intestine
Water is absorbed. The undigested food is mainly roughage (a form of cellulose). This adds bulk to the food and helps the peristaltic action throughout the canal.

In the rectum
The 'waste food' is collected and then passed out of the body through the anus.

How the Food Constituents are Digested and Absorbed

Proteins

These are acidified in the stomach. Digestion is begun by pepsin in the gastric juice which turns the proteins into peptones (a simpler form of protein).

In the small intestine, erepsin (in the intestinal juice) and tripsin (in the pancreatic juice) finally break down the peptones into amino acids. These are absorbed by the walls of the small intestine and enter the blood stream.

Fats

These are not digested in the mouth or stomach. The bile from the gall bladder is poured into the small intestine. This emulsifies the fats and makes them alkaline.

They are broken down by lipase from the pancreatic juice into fatty acids and glycerol. These are then absorbed through the walls of the small intestine, passing into the lymph and then into the blood stream.

Carbohydrates

Cooked starch is acted on by amylase (ptyalin) in the saliva and turned to maltose.

There is no digestion of carbohydrates in the stomach.

In the small intestine amylase (in the pancreatic juice) continues the turning of starch to maltose. Maltase, lactase and invertase (all in the intestinal juice) finally turn all the carbohydrates to glucose. This is absorbed by the walls of the small intestine and passes into the blood stream.

Vitamins, minerals and water need no digestion. They are mainly absorbed by the walls of the small intestine, and pass into the blood stream. Liquid, when swallowed alone, is absorbed by the walls of the stomach and intestines.

Roughage (cellulose) is not digested but passes right through the alimentary canal and then out of the body.

THREE

Foods which provide Animal Proteins

*Meat, fish, eggs, milk and cheese – Their composition,
structure and value in the diet – Action of cooking on these
foods – How to choose them.*

Meat

The term meat includes the flesh of slaughtered animals and birds,
e.g. cattle, pigs, sheep, chickens, ducks.

Classification

1. Muscular cuts from the muscles which cover the skeleton.

White meat: e.g. veal, rabbit, chicken, is of looser texture, and
contains less fat and connective tissue than

Red meat: e.g. beef, pork, lamb. This meat has more flavour.

There is little difference between the nutritive values of the two
types.

2. Offal – the term applied to organs of the animal's body;
they differ in structure according to the individual functions.

Composition of meat

Animal protein is provided by lean meat.

Fat is present in varying amounts.

Iron, potassium and phosphorus are found in all meat, especially in liver and kidney.

The vitamins present are: A in fat meat and liver: B complex
in all meat.

The coarser cuts are equal in food value to prime cuts but
require slow, moist, cooking.

Offal is a valuable addition to the diet.

Liver is an excellent source of protein, vitamin A, vitamins of
B complex and iron. (Cook liver very gently to render it easily
digestible.)

Kidney and heart are good sources of protein.

Brain, tripe and sweetbreads are also good sources of protein
and are very easily digested.

Structure of meat

Lean meat consists of bundles of muscle fibres which lie side by side, and which are held together by connective tissue. The bundles are joined to the bones by tendons. Each fibre is made up of cells containing the protein myosin and a watery solution of mineral salts, vitamins and extractives. These extractives give the flavour to the meat. The walls of the fibres are composed of the protein elastin, and the connective tissue of the protein collagen. Fat cells ('invisible' fat) are found in the connective tissue between the fibres. There are also special fat deposits ('visible' fat) in various parts of the animal's body, e.g. under the skin and around the internal organs.

How cooking affects meat

1. It improves flavour and appearance.
2. It destroys harmful parasites and bacteria.
3. The proteins of the muscle fibres coagulate, and the connective tissue is softened. If cooking is continued the fibres shrink and the juice is squeezed out. In dry heat the water evaporates and the extractives are left on the meat. In moist heat the connective tissue is turned to gelatine, which dissolves in the liquid and the muscle fibres fall apart. The fat melts and runs out of the meat.

Digestibility of meat

The flavour of cooked meat has a stimulating effect on the flow of gastric juice, thus aiding digestion.

Digestibility depends on the amount of fat present, the amount of connective tissue and the length of the muscle fibres. This latter depends on the amount of muscular work done by that part of the animal during life. Meat from young animals has shorter fibre and less connective tissue and is therefore more digestible.

Tenderness also depends on the length of time the meat is hung after slaughter. On hanging, certain acids develop which help to gelatinize the connective tissue.

How to choose meat

1. All lean meat must be firm and elastic to touch.
2. There must be no strong smell.
3. Meat must be moist but not wet.

4. Any fluid must be watery but not sticky.
5. *Beef:* the lean is dark red, and the fat is firm and yellow.
   Lamb: the lean is dull red, and the fat is hard and white.
   Pork: the lean is pale pink, and the fat is soft and white.
   Bacon: the lean is pink, and the fat is white.
   Veal: the lean is pale and soft, and there is very little fat.

For roasting, grilling and frying, the more expensive cuts which have shorter fibres and less connective tissue are required. These come from the parts of the animal which had little muscular movement when it was alive.

For boiling, stewing and braising, the cheaper cuts may be used, as these can be made tender by careful cooking.

Storage of meat at home

Food poisoning can be caused by careless handling and poor storage of meat products. There is danger of contamination from: (a) parasites; (b) harmful bacteria; (c) toxins formed by bacteria.

Raw meat: This should first be wiped with a clean, damp cloth. Keep cool, clean and covered (in a refrigerator), *or* hang in a cool airy place, protected from flies, *or* salt by immersing in brine or by rubbing in dry salt. Raw meat should not be kept for longer than 1–2 days in a cool larder, or 2–4 days in a refrigerator.

Offal: This should be placed in a non-airtight container or covered loosely and kept very cool. Offal should not be kept for longer than one day in a cool larder or 1–2 days in a refrigerator, as it is particularly liable to rapid spoilage.

Cooked meat: Cool quickly; store covered in a cool place. It should keep 1–2 days in a cool place and 3–4 days in a refrigerator.

Bacon: This should be wrapped loosely in greaseproof paper and kept in a covered container. It will keep 3–4 days in a cool larder or up to 7 days in a refrigerator.

The storage times given are only meant as a rough guide. They will depend on storage conditions before purchase, which are not always known, so commonsense should always prevail; if there is any doubt whatsoever about freshness, the meat should not be used.

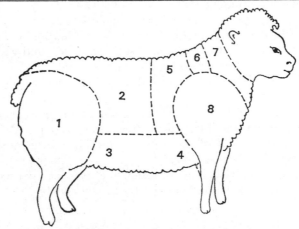

Fig. 3. Cuts of lamb and mutton, and how to cook them.

1. Leg to roast or boil.
2. Loin to roast, or to cut in chops to grill or fry.
3. Flank to stew.
4. Breast to stew.

5. Best end of neck to roast or to cut into cutlets to grill or fry.
6. Middle neck to stew.
7. Scrag end of neck to stew.
8. Shoulder to roast.

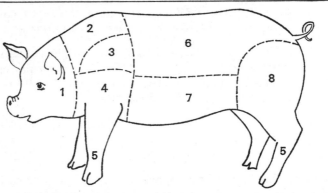

Fig. 4. Cuts of pork, and how to cook them.

1. Head to salt and boil and make into brawn.
2. Spare rib to roast or to cut into chops to grill or fry.
3. Blade to roast
4. Hand to roast or boil.

5. Foot to stew for brawn or trotters.
6. Loin to roast or to cut into chops to grill or fry.
7. Belly to boil, stew or pickle.
8. Leg to roast or to salt and boil.

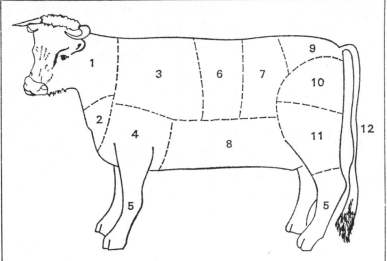

Fig. 5. Cuts of beef, and how to cook them.

1. Neck to stew.
2. Clod to stew.
3. Foreribs to roast.
4. Brisket to boil, salt and boil, or slow roast.
5. Shin to stew.
6. Wing-rib to roast.
7. Sirloin to roast.

8. Flank to salt and boil, or to stew.
9. Rump and fillet to roast, grill or fry.
10. Topside to roast.
11. Silverside to boil, or to salt and boil.
12. Oxtail to stew.

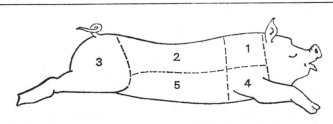

Fig. 6. Cuts of bacon.

1. Collar.
2. Back.
3. Gammon.

4. Hock.
5. Streaky.

SUITABLE CUTS OF MEAT FOR DIFFERENT METHODS OF COOKING

	LAMB AND MUTTON	BEEF	PORK	BACON
Roasting	Loin, leg, shoulder	Sirloin, ribs	Loin, leg	Ham, after par-boiling
Grilling and Frying	Loin-chops, cutlets	Fillet or rump steak	Loin-chops, spare-rib	Streaky or back rashers
Boiling	Sheep's head	Silverside	Belly	Hock, collar, gammon, ham
Stewing	Scrag end of neck	Shin, chucksteak, oxtail	Belly, hand	
Braising	Heart	Brisket		

Fish

Classification

1. *White fish:* These have all their fat stored in the liver, which is not usually eaten.

White fish can be: (*a*) round fish, e.g. whiting, cod. (*b*) flat fish, e.g. plaice, sole, turbot.

2. *Oily fish:* These have the fat distributed through the flesh which is therefore darker in colour, e.g. herring, mackerel, salmon.

3. *Shell fish:* These are protected by a hard external shell. They may be:

(*a*) Crustaceans, e.g. crab, lobster, crayfish.

(*b*) Molluscs (which live inside a bi-valvular shell), e.g. cockles, mussels, oysters. Shell fish have their fat stored in the liver.

Composition of fish

They all provide animal protein, vitamins of B complex, and valuable mineral substances (iodine, calcium and phosphorus). Oily fish provide fat, and the fat soluble vitamins A and D. The livers of white fish such as cod and halibut are valuable sources of these vitamins, and oils extracted from them are given to children and adults during winter months.

Structure of fish

The flesh consists of flakes made up of bundles of muscle fibres shorter than those of meat. These are held together by connective tissue consisting chiefly of collagen.

How cooking affects fish

It coagulates the muscle protein which later shrinks, squeezing out liquid containing water-soluble vitamins and minerals. The connective tissue collagen is changed to gelatine, and the fibres fall apart. Fat melts and runs out.

Digestibility of fish

White fish is very easily digested as it contains no fat and little connective tissue and the flakes are therefore easily broken apart during cooking. This class of fish is very suitable for invalids and young children.

Oily fish is slightly more difficult to digest as the fat is distributed through the flesh.

Shell fish such as crabs and lobsters are difficult to digest as the fibres are long and tough.

The use of fish in meal planning

1. As a useful alternative to meat in main meals. Many oily fish such as herrings, sprats and mackerel are an inexpensive source of animal protein.

2. If suitably cooked, fish can be given to infants and invalids.

3. It can be used for snack meals, e.g. sardines on toast.

4. It can be served cold with salad.

How to choose fish

1. There must be no unpleasant smell.

2. The flesh must be firm.

3. The tails must be stiff.

4. The gills must be red.

5. The eyes must be bright.

6. The scales on fish such as herrings must be plentiful.

7. The marking on plaice must be bright orange.

Storage of fish at home

Fresh fish is a highly perishable food and is best eaten on the day of purchase; it will keep till the following day in a refrigerator. To prevent the smell of fish pervading other foods in the refrigerator, it should be loosely covered and stored as high as possible.

Methods of cooking fish

Preparation: remove scales, entrails and fins of fish (and usually the head also). Wash well.

How

Why

(*a*) *Boiling:* Suitable for large fish.

Place fish into seasoned boiling water.

To retain the flavour, and to minimize the loss of soluble nutrients.

How	Why
Cover and simmer gently; allow 7–10 mins. per 500 g and 10 mins. over.	To avoid fish falling apart.
Use the fish stock for making sauce.	To avoid waste of soluble nutrients.

(b) *Steaming:* Suitable for any fish if not too large.

Place in a steamer, or between two plates over a pan of boiling water.	Fish is cooked by direct or by indirect heat.

(c) *Grilling:* Suitable for small whole fish, or for steaks or fillets.

Slash whole fish along back. Brush cutlets or fillets with fat or oil.	To allow heat to penetrate. To prevent them drying.
Place under hot grill, turn and watch carefully.	To prevent burning.

(d) *Baking:* Suitable for large fish or large cuts.

Prepare (this may include stuffing).	To improve flavour and food value.
Put dabs of fat on fish. Cook in a moderate oven (160°C, Mark 3) allowing 7–10 mins. per 500 g.	To prevent drying.

(e) *Frying:* Suitable for small fish, steaks or fillets.

Fry oily fish without adding fat.	Fat melts and runs out into pan from fish.
Coat white fish with egg and breadcrumbs, or batter, and fry in deep or shallow fat.	To form a protective covering to fish and prevent drying.

(f) *Sousing:* Suitable for herring and mackerel.

Place fish in casserole with vinegar, water, herbs and seasoning. Cover.	To add flavour and to keep fish moist.
Bake gently in a slow oven until soft.	To prevent fish breaking up.

Eggs

Structure

1. A porous shell, mainly of calcium carbonate.

2. Two shell membranes lying close together, and lining the shell, except at the large end of the egg, where they are separated and enclose the air space.

3. Egg white, consisting of a thick, sticky liquid (the albumen).

4. Egg yolk, surrounded by a thin membrane, which extends into the white as 'balancers' holding the yolk in position (the chalaza).

5. The embryo, inside the yolk membrane.

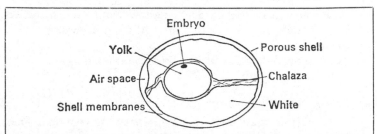

Fig. 7. Section of a hen's egg. The Shell consists of calcium carbonate. The White contains albumen and water, vitamin B₁ and mineral salts. The Yolk contains fat, protein, mineral salts and vitamins. The Chalaza holds the yolk in position.

Composition of eggs

The white contains animal protein albumen, with small quantities of mineral substances and riboflavin.

The yolk contains fat in an emulsified form; vitellin, a protein resembling albumen; mineral salts (calcium, phosphorus, iron and sulphur); vitamins A, B_1, B_2 and D.

Eggs contain about 75 per cent water.

How cooking affects eggs

The protein in the white coagulates at about 60°C and in the yolk at about 65°C.

The yolk remains softer than the white owing to the fat in it.

When egg dishes such as custards are overcooked, the egg shrinks, causing 'curdling'; the protein hardens and a watery fluid separates out.

Digestibility

Eggs are easily digested, because unlike meat or fish they have no tough connective tissue, and the fat is highly emulsified. They are therefore very suitable for invalids and young children.

Egg white is most easily digested when lightiy cooked.

How eggs may be used in cookery

1. As a main dish, supplying animal protein, e.g. scrambled, fried, poached or boiled.

2. To give flavour and colour to dishes, e.g. egg sauce.

3. To enrich cakes and puddings, e.g. added to milk puddings.

4. To enclose and retain air which acts as a raising agent, e.g. in whisked sponge cakes, hot soufflés.

5. To bind mixtures together, e.g. stuffings, fish cakes.

6. For coating foods for frying, either in a batter or with bread crumbs, e.g. fish fillets.

7. To thicken mixtures, e.g. custards, salad dressings.

8. To add nourishment to almost any beverage for those on a fluid diet.

9. As a glaze on pastry, scones, etc.

How to choose, store and preserve eggs

As the shell is porous, bacteria can enter from the air and cause the egg to decay. Test for freshness by:

(*a*) Holding to a strong light. There should be no solid patches.

(*b*) Placing in brine solution. If the egg is fresh it will sink, if stale it will float because gases have been produced inside the shell.

Store eggs in a cool dry place, away from strong smelling foods as they readily absorb odours. If stored in a refrigerator, remove them half an hour before use.

Preserve eggs by closing the shell pores to prevent air entering:

(*a*) By painting the shell with melted fat, or with a commercial solution, e.g. Oteg.

(*b*) By storing in a cold solution of sodium silicate (water glass).

Milk

Composition

Milk contains most of the essential nutrients:

Protein: 3 per cent animal protein (caseinogen, lactalbumin, lactoglobulin).

Carbohydrate: 5 per cent as lactose or milk sugar.

Fat: 4 per cent in the form of a fine emulsion.

Mineral substances: 1 per cent, chiefly calcium, phosphorus, sodium, potassium and traces of iron.

Vitamins: A, D, B_2 (and a little B_1, B_3 and C).

Water: 87 per cent.

Milk helps to maintain the bacteria in the large intestine which act on the mass of waste residue collecting there to produce certain vitamins of the B complex, supplementing the body's supply. The production of lactic acid from lactose also discourages the growth of putrefactive bacteria.

How milk is made safe to drink

Milk is an ideal breeding ground for all bacteria. It can become contaminated with harmful organisms at any time during its journey from cow to consumer, e.g. from a diseased cow, or from any person who deals with it in transit, or from contaminated water or equipment. The precautions taken are:

1. To ensure that the cows are healthy, and no contamination arises from the dairies, the dairy workers, or their equipment.

2. To cool the milk rapidly after milking.

3. To treat the milk by heating it to destroy bacteria, either
(*a*) by sterilizing at not less than 100°C for $\frac{1}{2}$ to 1 hour to destroy all organisms or
(*b*) by pasteurizing at 72°C for 15 seconds, to reduce the number of micro-organisms.

Pasteurizing and sterilization do not alter the nutritive value of the milk, except by reducing the vitamin C content. They do slightly alter the taste.

How heating affects milk

Heating causes the coagulation of two of the proteins in milk, the lactalbumin and the lactoglobulin, but it does not coagulate the caseinogen. The coagulated proteins form a skin on the surface of the milk, at about 60°C. When heating is continued, bubbles of steam form under this skin and cause the milk to boil over.

Digestibility

Milk is easily digested by most people.

Rennin in the stomach causes coagulation of the caseinogen. The clots of casein so formed in the stomach are made smaller, and digestibility improved by:

(a) Boiling the milk,

(b) Taking it with a cereal food,

(c) Adding soda water.

Uses of milk

Milk is a fairly cheap food, and a particularly cheap source of protein. Because it is both highly nutritious and easily digestible, it is of great use in the feeding of babies, invalids, expectant and nursing mothers, old people and adolescents. Milk has a bland taste, which enables it to be used in a variety of ways, thus avoiding monotony in the diet:

1. *Beverages:* plain or flavoured as milk shakes, cocoa, etc.
2. *With cereals:* breakfast cereals, milk puddings, porridge, etc.
3. *In soups and sauces* both sweet and savoury.
4. *In puddings* such as custards, junkets, milk jellies.
5. *In flour mixtures* such as batters, cakes, etc.

Why milk goes sour

Lactic acid bacteria are always present in milk. In warm conditions these multiply rapidly and act on the lactose turning it to lactic acid. This acid causes the milk to clot (i.e. separate into curds and whey) – it also causes the sour taste. The curds or solid part contain the casein and fat and some mineral salts; the whey contains the lactalbumin, lactoglobulin, mineral salts and the remaining lactose (milk sugar).

Storage of milk at home

Keep it cool, clean and covered:

Cool by storing in a refrigerator or in a cool place. In hot weather it can be covered with muslin which hangs into a dish of cold water. As the water evaporates, it cools the milk.

Clean by keeping in bottles or cartons until required, and by sterilizing milk jugs.

Covered by keeping in bottles or cartons, or by covering jugs with muslin to exclude dust and flies.

Milk products

Cream rises to the top of milk and contains mainly fat, water and vitamins A and D.

Butter is made by churning cream after it has been ripened by the action of bacteria. Butter contains fat, water, vitamins A and D and some mineral substances.

Cheese

The composition of cheese

This, of course, varies according to the type of cheese and the milk from which it is made. Approximately 50 g of cheese can be made from 500 ml of milk, and contains most of the milk proteins and fats.

On the average, cheese contains: $\frac{1}{3}$ protein; $\frac{1}{3}$ fat; $\frac{1}{3}$ water together with calcium, phosphorus, added salt and vitamin A.

The type of cheese depends on:

(*a*) The type of milk (cow's, goat's or ewe's).

(*b*) The composition of the milk (whole or skimmed).

(*c*) The acid or rennet used for clotting.

(*d*) The pressure applied during making.

(*e*) The changes during the ripening process due to enzymes, bacteria and moulds.

How cheese is made

(*a*) *In the home, from soured milk:* the lactic acid produced when milk sours causes the coagulation of the milk proteins. The curd is then separated from the whey by straining through muslin. The milk cheese is then seasoned, and may also be flavoured with chives, parsley, etc. The resulting product is known as cottage cheese, and may be made from milk which has had the cream removed, i.e. skimmed milk.

(*b*) *Commercially:* commercially the milk is separated into curds and whey by the action of special cultures of bacteria, by heat, and by rennet. The curd is separated from the whey, salted, and pressed as dry as possible. It is then allowed to ripen in a cool place so that the characteristic flavour develops owing to the action of bacteria and moulds. Some commercial cheese is made from whole milk, some from skimmed milk, and some from milk containing a high percentage of cream. The type of milk used determines the fat content of the finished cheese.

Processed cheese

This is made from Cheddar type cheese by grinding it to a pulp, or melting it with milk in steam heated containers. This pasteurizes the cheese which is then cooled, moulded and packed.

How cooking affects cheese

The fat melts and the cheese softens. If heating is continued, the protein hardens, shrinks and squeezes out the fat. In this state it is difficult to digest.

Digestibility

Some people find it difficult to digest, but the digestibility can be improved by:

(*a*) Chopping or grating finely.

(*b*) Mixing with starchy foods such as potatoes or macaroni, or with flour in a cheese sauce (the starch will absorb some of the melted fat).

(*c*) Serving with mustard or vinegar (these help stimulate the digestive juices).

(*d*) Avoiding overcooking, as this causes the protein to shrink and harden.

The use of cheese in the diet

Cheese has a high food value and is a valuable food. It is a way of preserving the food value of milk – which does not itself keep – in a concentrated form. It can be used in a variety of ways:

1. As the main dish to provide protein. Useful for vegetarians, in macaroni cheese, cheese pie, etc.

2. As a snack meal, e.g. Welsh rarebit, cheese and biscuits.

3. As a savoury course at the end of a meal.

4. As a flavouring, e.g. sauces, or sprinkled on to soups or salads, or as a sandwich filling.

How to store cheese

(*a*) In a refrigerator if well wrapped, or in a closed container, to prevent it from drying, or from tainting other foods.

(*b*) Wrap in greaseproof paper or hang in a muslin bag, and keep in a cool place.

FOUR

Foods which provide Plant Proteins

Cereals, nuts and pulses – Wheat products – Types of flour.

Plant proteins are found in cereals, pulses and nuts. They are less valuable than animal proteins as they have one or more of the essential amino acids missing. For this reason they are known also as incomplete, or (rarely now) second-class, proteins. They are however of great value when combined with even small quantities of animal protein, and they can be used as the sole source of protein in a strict vegetarian diet. Starch is usually present in larger quantities than the protein in these plant foods.

Cereals

These are the edible seeds of certain plants, e.g. wheat, maize, barley, oats. A great variety of foods is produced from these plants, e.g. flour, cornflour, macaroni, spaghetti, semolina, breakfast cereals.

Why cereals are important in our diet
　1. Their growth is widespread, and many parts of the earth can produce one or more cereal plants.
　2. They are easily preserved when the seeds are ripe, and easily transported.
　3. They are inexpensive compared with animal protein foods.
　4. They are easy to prepare and to digest.
　5. They have no strong taste and can be made pleasant to eat in a variety of ways.
　6. They all contain starch; many also contain fat, mineral substances and vitamins of B complex as well as protein.

How cereals are used for our food
　1. As a staple item of diet, e.g. bread in Europe, rice in Asia and maize in Southern U.S.A.

2. As a breakfast dish (e.g. porridge) or processed into prepared cereals. Flaked cereals are made by rolling the coarsely ground endosperm and then cooking it. Puffed cereals are prepared by heating the grains under pressure and then suddenly releasing the pressure so that the steam inside the grain expands rapidly, thus puffing up the grain.

3. As the essential ingredient in cooking cakes, pastries and many puddings.

4. As a thickening agent in soups, sauces and gravies.

How cooking affects cereals

When cooked by moist heat:

(*a*) The cellulose is softened.

(*b*) The starch grains swell, burst and absorb liquid.

(*c*) The protein coagulates.

(*d*) The flavour is developed and the cereal becomes more digestible.

When cooked by dry heat:

The starch grains swell and the starch is turned to dextrin. If heating is continued the starch and protein burn.

The chief cereals used for food

Oats: These supply much energy because they contain fat. They have a high protein content but no gluten (see page 49). Oats are ground to a fine, medium or coarse meal, or rolled to form flakes. They are used for porridge, oatcakes, for thickening soups and stews and for coating food for frying.

Barley: This is used for making malt in brewing. Barley in the household is used in small grains known as pearl barley, made by polishing the kernels after removing the husk. It may also be ground to a fine powder as patent barley. Either form may be used to prepare barley water, a cool and refreshing drink. Pearl barley is added to soups and stews.

Maize: When young and fresh, maize may be cooked as a vegetable and eaten as corn on the cob. When ripe the endosperm may be ground to form cornflour, and used as the basis of custard powder, etc., or it may be coarsely ground and rolled to prepare breakfast cereals. Diets which depend on maize as the staple food tend to be deficient in vitamin B_3, leading to the deficiency disease pellagra.

Rice: Rice is one of the least nutritious of cereals, containing the most starch and the least protein, fat and minerals. The bran and germ of unpolished rice contain vitamin B_1 and minerals, but polished rice has had these removed. The polished rice grains are sometimes parboiled and dried before polishing; this processing causes a little of the vitamin B complex to be absorbed by the endosperm.

From the time rice is harvested, therefore, it is unfortunately subjected to a series of treatments – such as milling and polishing – which seriously deplete it of its nutrients. For example, 600 g husked rice (2,200 Calories) will provide 52 g protein, but a similar quantity of polished rice provides only 37 g. Where the diet consists of very little else, this difference can be crucial. Bad storage, washing and cooking it in excessive water will diminish the nutritive value of rice even more. Other important deficiencies in typical rice diets are in the B group vitamins, vitamin A and calcium.

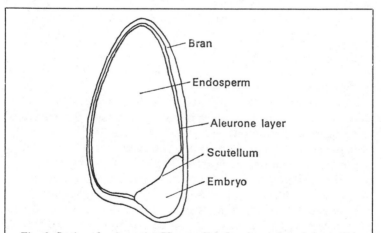

Fig. 8. Section of a rice grain. The unpolished grain consists of about 78% carbohydrate, 11% moisture, 7½% protein and 2% oil, with small amounts of B group vitamins, calcium and iron present. When the seedcoat and germ is removed (as with polished rice) the protein content is diminished and there is scarcely any vitamin content left.

Rice may be bought in the form of grains (long grained or Patna rice is used chiefly for savoury dishes, as the grains may be boiled in water and easily separated without forming a starchy mass. Short grained rice is used chiefly for milk puddings). Rice is also ground to a powder and sold as ground rice, for use in puddings, cake mixtures, etc.

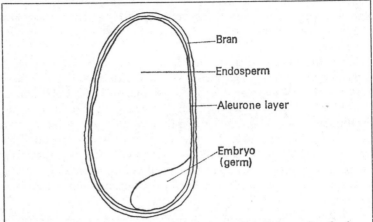

Fig. 9. Section of a wheat grain. The bran contains cellulose, mineral salts and vitamins of B complex. The embryo contains fat, protein and vitamins of B complex. The scutellum contains vitamin B_1. The aleurone layer contains protein. The endosperm contains starch and a little protein.

Wheat: Wheat grain consists of:

13 per cent bran on the outside made of several thin layers containing cellulose, a little protein, iron, calcium, phosphorus and vitamins of B complex.

85 per cent endosperm consisting of thin walled cells containing starch grains separated by protein. The aleurone layer is the single celled layer of endosperm nearest to the bran, and contains mostly protein with some fat, minerals and vitamins of B complex.

2 per cent embryo, rich in proteins, fat, minerals and vitamins. The scutellum lies between the endosperm and the embryo, and contains enzymes, mineral substances and vitamins.

The chief use of wheat in Britain is for the production of flour.

How flour is made

(*a*) The grains of wheat are cleaned.

(*b*) They are put through rollers which split them, releasing the endosperm and breaking the outside layer of the grain into flakes.

(c) This mixture, finely ground, produces wholemeal flour, i.e. a flour which contains all the nutrients of the wheat.

(d) If the germ and bran are removed after rolling and the remainder (chiefly endosperm) is ground, white flour is produced. The miller adds to this calcium, iron and the vitamins B_1 and B_3 to replace those lost in the bran and germ. The flour has an off-white colour. It keeps well and is digestible, as the roughage of the bran has been removed.

Types of wheat flour

Different types of flour contain different amounts of protein. When mixed with water in a dough, the proteins form a sticky elastic substance known as gluten. This gluten can hold the starch grains, fat globules and gases. When heated, the elastic gluten is stretched by the expanding gases and later, being a protein, is 'set' or coagulated to form the framework of the cooked mixture.

A 'strong' flour is made from hard wheat grown in extreme climates and contains from 10–15 per cent gluten; it has high rising properties and absorbs a large amount of liquid. It is best for all yeast mixtures and for puff pastry.

A 'weak' or soft flour contains from 8–10 per cent gluten and is made from softer more starchy wheat grown in a milder climate. This flour is more suitable for cakes, biscuits and short crust pastry.

A blended flour is a mixture of strong and weak flours, and is usually sold as plain flour, i.e. with no raising agent added. A self-raising flour has a raising agent already incorporated in it. The amount is usually that required to raise a plain cake mixture. It has the advantage of convenience, but the disadvantage that the amount of raising agent cannot be varied.

Other wheat products supplying protein

Semolina is made from coarsely milled hard wheat and is used for puddings and thickening soups.

Macaroni, spaghetti, vermicelli and other 'pasta' foods are made from strong flour which is first made into a paste with water. The high gluten content enables the paste to be moulded into different shapes or into long threads or tubes. These are dried and partially cooked. They are used for dishes with meat or cheese, or for puddings.

Pulses and Nuts

Pulses

These are the dried seeds of leguminous plants. They are a cheap source of protein and are particularly useful in vegetarian diets. They are also widely used in countries where animal protein is unavailable, or too expensive. Pulses such as peas, beans and lentils also provide carbohydrates, minerals and small amounts of vitamins of the B complex. Since they must be soaked before cooking to soften them the same water should be used in the cooking process, so that the water soluble vitamins are not lost.

Peanuts (groundnuts) are not really nuts but pulses. They are a rich source of protein and fat. Crushed peanuts are often used as peanut butter, a spread for bread. In countries where they form an important part of the diet they are often cooked in a kind of stew.

Soya flour is produced from the fruit of another leguminous plant, the soya bean. It is rich in protein and fat, as well as carbohydrate, calcium, iron and vitamins of the B complex. In fact, though vegetable, soya is a complete protein. This makes it a very valuable food for poor or underdeveloped countries, and is why it can be used in the production of substitute meat'.

Nuts

Nuts, in which we include almonds, walnuts, cashews, Brazils, sweet chestnuts, hazels, cobs, pecans and pistachios form another valuable food. Their protein content is similar to that of dried peas and beans but, as they are not soaked before cooking, weight for weight they are a richer source of vegetable protein. They also contain fat, carbohydrate, some mineral salts and vitamins of the B complex.

Nuts contain a large amount of roughage and are therefore difficult to digest unless they are chewed well. They may be minced or ground before being used. They are used largely in vegetarian dishes, in stuffings, in cakes and sweets, or served as a dessert.

FIVE

Foods which provide Carbohydrates
Starchy foods not already dealt with – Bread – Sugar –
Fruits and vegetables – The cooking of vegetables –
Salads – Their importance in the diet.

Starch

(For wheat products, oats, barley, maize and rice see Chapter 4.)
Other sources of starch are:

Sago: This is made from the pith of the sago palm.

Tapioca: This is from the roots of the cassava plant.

Arrowroot: This is made from the underground stem of maranta.

They are used mainly for milk puddings, for thickening soups, sauces and drinks.

Bread

Why bread is an important food:

1. It is reasonably cheap.

2. It has no strong flavour and can be eaten with a wide variety of other foods.

3. It is easily digested, white bread probably more easily than wholemeal owing to absence of roughage.

4. It is one of the main sources of Calories in the average diet. It contains 60 per cent of carbohydrate and about 8 per cent of protein. The protein content is important as bread is a standard item of diet.

5. Mineral salts and vitamins B_1 and B_3 are present in the wholemeal flour. Iron, calcium and vitamins are added by millers to the white flour. Some calcium and iron in wholemeal bread may be unavailable owing to the presence of phytic acid with which they form insoluble salts.

How bread is used

1. As a staple item of most diets with butter, margarine or other spreads.

2. In snack meals as sandwiches, savouries on toast, etc.

3. In puddings such as bread and butter pudding, summer pudding, apple charlotte, etc.

4. As toast and rusks.

5. As breadcrumbs in stuffings, steamed puddings, etc. or as a coating for fried foods or sprinkled on 'au gratin' dishes.

Types of bread

1. White bread made from 72 per cent extraction flour fortified during milling (72 per cent flour extracted from the wheat).

2. Wholemeal bread made from 85–90 per cent extraction flour containing more roughage and fat, and having more flavour.

3. Milk breads containing dried skimmed milk.

4. Breads enriched with germ of wheat or malt and so containing extra vitamins and minerals.

5. Starch-reduced breads made from flours from which much of the starch has been removed.

Sugars

Glucose is made commercially from starch. It is a mild sweetening agent and is used as a quick energy food as it requires no digestion and is rapidly absorbed into the blood stream.

Sucrose is produced from sugar cane, and from sugar beet. It is present in all ripe and dried fruits.

How sugar is made

1. The beets or canes are crushed and the sugar extracted with water.

2. This is purified by adding lime and bubbling carbon dioxide through it.

3. The liquid is evaporated and crystals of brown sugar form. The liquid left is molasses or treacle.

4. The crystals are dissolved and again purified and bleached.

5. The liquid is again evaporated and crystals of white sugar are formed. The liquid left is golden syrup.

Types of sugar in common use

1. *Lump or loaf sugar.* This is compressed and cut into even-sized lumps.

2. *Granulated sugar* consists of coarse crystals suitable for sweetening dishes in cooking.

3. *Caster sugar* consists of finer crystals and is suitable for cake making because it dissolves readily, and also for sprinkling over sweet dishes.

4. *Icing sugar* is very finely ground sugar and is used for all icing mixtures and for sprinkling over cakes.

5. *Demerara sugar* is less refined and is therefore a light brown in colour. It consists of coarse crystals.

6. *Moist brown sugar* is even less refined. It has smaller crystals, is a dark brown colour and contains more moisture and molasses.

Treacle and syrup are by-products in the refining of sugar. They contain some invert sugar (i.e. monosaccharides – see Chapter 1) which inhibits crystallization of the sucrose. Treacle also contains valuable mineral substances. They are used in cake and pudding making and as spreads on bread.

Honey contains about 75 per cent invert sugar as well as some sucrose. Jams supply us with sucrose (added during the cooking) and some invert sugar formed during boiling.

Fruits

Fruits are seed-bearing parts of plants; during ripening they become fleshy, succulent and sweet.

Why fruit is an important food

1. When fruits are formed, food reserves are laid down as starches and pectin, and as the fruits ripen the starch is changed to sugars.

2. They contain mineral substances; chiefly potassium, phosphorus, calcium, manganese and a little iron.

3. They supply roughage especially in the skins and seeds.

4. All fruits supply water, some, like melon, as much as 94 per cent.

5. Most fruits supply vitamin C, but some such as the citrus fruits are particularly rich in this. In addition, all orange-coloured fruits, such as oranges, apricots, peaches, bananas and rose hips, supply carotene which the body can change into vitamin A.

6. Fruits also contain organic acids which form the salts which give them their individual flavour, and which also help to maintain the natural alkalinity of the body fluids.

How fruit is used
1. As a raw dessert. Crisp fruit is useful for cleansing the teeth.
2. As preserves in jam, jelly, marmalade and chutney.
3. As cooked fruit either stewed, baked or fried.
4. Combined with flour mixtures, e.g. pastry, batters.
5. In cold sweets, e.g. fruit fools, salads, mousses, jellies.
6. Dried fruits, e.g. sultanas, raisins, currants, give variety to cakes and puddings.

How cooking affects fruit
1. The cellulose framework is softened.
2. Owing to the acidity of fruit there is only a little destruction of vitamin C.
3. Soluble nutrients pass into the cooking liquid, but as this is generally served, there is no loss.

Vegetables

Vegetables are usually classified according to the part of the plant from which they come:
 (*a*) *Roots*, e.g. carrots, turnips.
 (*b*) *Bulbs*, e.g. onions, shallots.
 (*c*) *Tubers*, e.g. potatoes, Jerusalem artichokes, yams.
 (*d*) *Stems*, e.g. celery, leeks.
 (*e*) *Leaves*, e.g. cabbage, sprouts.
 (*f*) *Flowers*, e.g. cauliflower, flowering broccoli.
 (*g*) *Fruits*, e.g. tomatoes, cucumbers, marrows.
 (*h*) *Seeds*, e.g. peas, broad beans.

Why vegetables are important in our diet
1. They provide valuable vitamins, e.g.
Carotene in red and yellow vegetables can be turned by the body to vitamin A and stored in the liver.
Some of the vitamins of B complex are present in potatoes, in green vegetables and in pulses.
Vitamin C is present in all green vegetables, in potatoes and in most salad vegetables. Care is necessary in preparation and in cooking to preserve this vitamin.
2. They provide valuable amounts of mineral salts such as

potassium, calcium, phosphorus, magnesium, iron and, in some cases, iodine.

3. The large amount of cellulose is useful to the body as roughage.

4. When young, vegetables such as onions, carrots and peas contain sugar, and potatoes and the leguminous vegetables contain starch. These carbohydrates supply energy and heat.

5. Some vegetables such as peas, beans and lentils supply valuable amounts of protein.

6. All vegetables supply water. Most contain from 70–95 per cent.

7. They supply variety in colour, flavour and texture in the diet.

How vegetables are used in our diet

1. As an accompaniment to the main protein foods, e.g. potatoes, root and green vegetables and salads with meat.

2. As the main part of a vegetarian meal, often with added protein foods: vegetable hotpot, vegetable pie, etc.

3. As the main ingredient in soups, or as purées for infants and invalids.

4. As preserves in pickles and chutneys.

5. As garnishes, and as flavouring for sauces.

Cooking of vegetables

The aim is:

(*a*) To preserve in the vegetable all the food value, paying particular attention to those food nutrients which are soluble in water or are destroyed by heat, e.g. mineral salts and vitamins B and C.

(*b*) To make them more palatable and digestible. During cooking the cellulose framework is softened, starch grains burst and are gelatinized.

(*c*) To cook vegetables when as fresh as possible, while they are at their best for taste and food value.

Preparation

Vegetables must be washed thoroughly to remove dirt, insects, etc., but should not be soaked, as vitamin C, the mineral salts and sugar are all soluble in water. An exception to this rule may be made in the case of potatoes. After peeling they should be kept in water until cooked, as enzymes in them cause browning on exposure to air.

Potatoes – scrape or peel thinly (unless cooking in the skin).

Root vegetables and onions – remove the outside skin thinly.

Pulses are easier to cook if soaked.

Frozen vegetables require no preparation and are usually of good quality as they are processed when at their best.

Choice of method

Choose a method suitable for the type of vegetable, using the conservative method where possible (i.e. one which conserves the food values), e.g. cook potatoes in jackets, cook green vegetables and roots in little water and as quickly as possible.

The conservative method of cooking green and root vegetables

How	Why
1. Prepare and cut the vegetables into small pieces; shred cabbage.	For quick cooking.
2. Put in pan about 2 cm depth of water; bring to boil.	Less water means less loss of soluble nutrients.
3. Add vegetables and a little salt.	To add flavour.
4. Cover with fitting lid and bring back to boil. Boil gently for about 10 minutes.	To prevent evaporation. To cook thoroughly.
5. Strain off liquid and use for soup or gravy.	To save nutrients which have dissolved in the water.
6. Serve vegetables at once.	To prevent loss of vitamin C.

They should be soft but *not* soggy.

Boiling is suitable for root vegetables and potatoes. Cover with water and cook gently so that they do not break into pieces.

Steaming is also suitable for roots and potatoes. There is no loss of soluble nutrients, as the vegetable does not touch the water.

This method is not suitable for green vegetables: the long cooking necessary spoils the colour and destroys vitamin C.

Stewing or braising is suitable for roots and onions. All soluble nutrients are retained. Carrots etc. may be cooked in an oven casserole.

Frying, baking and roasting are suitable for potatoes and some roots. Vitamin C is destroyed but there is no loss of soluble salts.

Grilling is suitable for vegetables which soften easily, e.g. tomatoes and mushrooms.

Salads

A salad is a mixture of vegetables or fruits, or sometimes both. The ingredients may be cooked but are more often served raw.

Why salads are served

(a) To supply vitamins, chiefly A and C, found in green vegetables, tomatoes and carrots, etc.

(b) To supply mineral salts, chiefly calcium, potassium, iron and phosphorus.

(c) To supply roughage. If served raw, vegetables must be young and tender.

(d) To give variety to meals in colour, texture and taste.

Salads are not usually a good source of Calories but these may be supplied by a good salad dressing. Protein is often added in the form of meat, eggs, cheese or nuts.

Strong flavours must be used sparingly, e.g. onions, garlic, chives.

Types of salads

(a) Those using raw green vegetables, e.g. lettuce, cress, chopped cabbage, sliced cucumber, together with coloured vegetables such as tomatoes, radishes, grated carrot, etc.

(b) Those using cooked vegetables, e.g. potato salad, Russian salad or mixed diced-vegetable salad.

(c) Those using a mixture of fruits, cooked or uncooked and served as a sweet.

(d) Those using a mixture of fruit and vegetables, e.g. orange, lettuce and watercress.

The making of salads

How	Why
1. Have all ingredients fresh.	They then have maximum food value.
2. Wash but do not soak.	To clean but to avoid loss of soluble nutrients.
3. Serve immediately they are prepared.	To avoid loss of vitamins.
4. Avoid shredding too finely unless vegetables are coarse.	Enzymes are set free. These destroy the vitamins.
5. Arrange attractively. A flat dish gives the best display.	To encourage appetite.
6. Serve with a suitable dressing.	To supply additional food nutrients.

Dressings

(*a*) *A French dressing* of oil and vinegar, or oil and lemon juice, is served with green salads. The green leaves may be tossed in the dressing just before serving, or dressing may be served separately.

(*b*) *A mayonnaise* made of egg yolks and oil may be served with any vegetable salad. This supplies fat and protein.

(*c*) *A cooked salad dressing* is often made by flavouring a thin white sauce. This may be served separately or used to coat eggs or fish served in the salad.

Fruit salads

These may contain any fruit in season, or tinned or bottled fruit. The fruit may be raw or cooked, but must be cut into neat even-sized pieces. It is served in a syrup of sugar and water, and often accompanied by cream, ice-cream, junket or custard.

The success of a fruit salad depends upon the skilful blending of colour and flavour.

SIX

Foods which provide Fats
Animal and vegetable fats – Food value – Use of fats.

Fats and oils are found both in plants and animals. Plants make them from starches and sugars; animals make them from fat in their food and also from carbohydrate foods.

Animal fats are obtained from meat, fish, milk and milk products. Vegetable fats are obtained from fruits and seeds, e.g. olives, nuts.

Why these foods are included in our meals

1. To supply the body with fat and fat-soluble vitamins.

2. To enable us to produce fried and roasted foods.

3. To make dry foods (e.g. bread) more palatable and easy to eat.

4. To improve the texture of flour doughs, i.e. as shorteners, in pastry and cakes.

Common fats

1. *Cream:* obtained by allowing milk to stand. The fat globules slowly rise to the top and are skimmed by hand or separated in a centrifuge. Cream may contain 20–50 per cent fat. Cream supplies fat in a palatable and easily digested form, together with fat soluble vitamins A and D. It may be served with pies, fruit, etc. It may be whipped, so enclosing air, until it is thick.

Clotted cream is produced from milk which is heated very slowly while the cream rises to the top. Cream substitutes may be made by emulsifying butter or margarine with milk.

2. *Butter:* cream is pasteurized and then allowed to ripen by the action of bacteria which cause it to develop certain character-istic flavours and a degree of acidity which breaks up the emul-sion; the fat globules then cling together. The mixture is churned to separate the liquid or buttermilk. Salt is added and the butter 'worked' until it is smooth in texture.

3. *Margarine:* oils from ground nuts, palm fruit, palm kernel,

coconuts or whale oil are purified and hydrogenated so that they make a solid fat. This is mixed with milk and salt and vitamins A and D are added. The mixture is then churned to make it of the consistency of butter.

Both butter and margarine contain about 85 per cent fat, and vitamins A and D. Margarine may have a percentage of butter added to improve its flavour, and the food value is very similar to that of butter. Both may be used for the same cooking processes, but the water present makes them rather unsuitable for frying.

4. *Synthetic cooking fats:* these are made from vegetable oils or whale oil and are purified and hydrogenated to give a white, solid fat. This has air incorporated into it, giving it a creamy texture. They may be used for pastry making or for frying.

5. *Animal cooking fats:*

(*a*) *Lard* is 100 per cent fat and is obtained from the pig. It is good for frying, it rubs easily into flour, but it does not cream well with sugar.

(*b*) *Suet* is a hard fat obtained from mutton or beef. It is usually taken from round the internal organs. It is chopped or grated and used for suet pastry, puddings, stuffings, etc.

(*c*) *Dripping* is the melted fat obtained when meat is roasted. Its flavour varies with the animal from which it is obtained.

6. *Oils:* edible oils are liquid fats, similar in food value to fats but with lower melting points (at normal room temperature they are in the liquid state). They may be used for frying, salad dressing and for cake and pastry making. The chief cooking oils are obtained from olives, maize, groundnuts and palm kernels. Oils obtained from the liver of white fish are rich sources of vitamin A and D, and are often given to children and invalids.

How to render fat

This is to extract fat from meat tissues to use as dripping. Cut the fat meat into small pieces, place in a dish in a slow oven until fat has melted. It may then be poured off and used.

How to clarify or clean fat

Place the fat in a strong pan and cover it with water. Heat gently until the water is boiling. Pour into a basin. When cool remove the fat from the top and scrape the bottom of the solid fat to remove impurities. Heat the fat gently until all bubbling stops: the residual water will have then evaporated. Cool.

How to store fats and oils

Fats may be turned rancid by the action of bacteria which break up the fat into fatty acids and glycerol. This may be prevented by storing the fat at a low temperature, wrapped in greaseproof paper. Oils should be stored in stoppered bottles at room temperature. If kept very cold they will of course solidify.

SEVEN

Meal Planning
General principles – Balanced menus – Shopping and budgeting – Meal planning for special groups – Meals for special occasions – Economy in catering – Réchauffé dishes – Convenience foods – Time planning.

In order to maintain good health a diet must

(*a*) Provide sufficient calories for all energy needs, and

(*b*) Contain the essential nutrients in adequate amounts, i.e. it must be 'balanced'.

A satisfactory diet must also be digestible, palatable, varied, reasonable in cost and acceptable to individual taste.

(*a*) *Calorie needs* (see also Chapter 1)

The correct Calorie allowance is one on which the body maintains its optimal weight or rate of growth. If too little food is eaten the body will stop growing or will lose weight. If too much is eaten the excess is stored as fat. In normal health, hunger is a guide to the amount needed, and the number of Calories required varies with age, sex, size and the amount of physical activity undertaken. For example, an old person requires fewer Calories because his basal metabolism has slowed down, and he is less active physically. A school child who is growing rapidly needs more food than an adult who is doing sedentary work, and all manual workers need still more Calories to provide energy for physical activity.

(*b*) *The balanced diet*

Calories can be supplied by fats, carbohydrates and proteins, but the proteins are the only nutrient which can be used to build body tissue. They are present mostly in the more expensive foods, and it is therefore wasteful to depend upon proteins for the Calorie requirements of the body, as these Calories can be equally well supplied by the cheaper fats and carbohydrates. Extra protein foods are always needed for children, adolescents, expectant and nursing mothers and for convalescents. Vitamins and mineral salts are next in importance to proteins for maintaining healthy growth. Thirst will indicate whether the body is receiving enough water. Some foods containing roughage should also be included to guard against constipation.

(c) Palatability and digestibility

Food which is appetizing in appearance, is neatly and colourfully served, and has an appetizing smell and a pleasant taste, will encourage appetite. This will cause a flow of saliva and gastric juices and will therefore aid digestion. Variety in the colour, texture and taste of the food will all help easy digestion, as will freedom from worry or emotional upset.

(d) Cost

An adequate and well balanced diet is not necessarily expensive, but a knowledge of food values, and of the best methods of cookery and careful budgeting are all needed to provide good meals at a reasonable cost. More money must be spent by someone who is out all day than by one who has time to spend on the preparation of less expensive foods.

(e) Individual taste and customs

Some people are allergic to certain foods which therefore must not be included in their diet. Customs of race, religion and family must also be considered. The 'pattern' of the meals may vary with the parents' occupation and habits, and the age of the children, or it may be just a matter of personal preference. Most family meals consist of either *(a)* Breakfast, dinner, light tea and supper, or *(b)* Breakfast, dinner, high tea and a snack before bedtime. The time of the main meal must depend upon the habits of the household, and if all the members are out all day it is often taken in the evening.

(f) Time at the disposal of the cook

This is an important consideration today when so many people are away from their own homes all day. They require to use ingenuity in planning, and time-saving foods such as frozen and tinned goods. The busy person will make use of ready prepared vegetables, deep-freeze foods, commercial cake mixes, etc., in spite of their relatively higher cost. Much time can be saved by making a 'basic' mixture which can be used for several different dishes, e.g. 500 g of short-crust pastry will be sufficient for a fruit pie for dinner, jam tarts for tea and savoury patties for the next day. From a rich cake mixture the housewife can make a large cake, small cakes of a different flavour and a steamed pudding.

With a refrigerator it is possible to store such things as pastry and yeast doughs for several days, and dry mixes of scones, plain cakes, etc. for longer periods. When they are needed it is only necessary to add liquid to these dry mixes, and to cook them.

(g) Time of the year and climate
The diet must be adjusted to external conditions. In cold weather extra Calories are needed to maintain body temperature. In hot weather lighter meals such as salads are usually preferred.

The Balanced Diet:
What Foods to Include and Why

Certain foods should be included in the daily diet of the normal healthy adult.

How	Why
500 ml milk. ½–1 litre for a child.	To supply animal protein, fat, milk-sugar, vitamins A, B_2, D, calcium and phosphorus.
50–100 g cooked meat or fish; liver occasionally.	To supply animal proteins, fat, vitamins of B complex, iron and calcium.
1 egg.	To supply protein, fat, vitamins, iron.
50 g cheese, nuts, pulses or additional meat.	To supply additional protein, vitamins, etc.
250 g bread, preferably wholemeal.	To supply carbohydrate, protein, iron, calcium and vitamins B_1 and B_3.

How	Why
1 serving of potato.	
1 serving of green or yellow vegetable.	To supply carbohydrate, roughage, minerals, vitamins A and C.
1 serving of another vegetable, preferably uncooked.	
1 serving of fruit.	
50 g butter or margarine.	To supply fat and vitamins A and D.

About $1\frac{1}{2}$ litres water in tea, coffee or other beverage.

It will be seen that the following rules will ensure that the nutrient named in each case is adequately supplied:

1. *Protein:* include meat, eggs, cheese, fish, milk, pulses or nuts.
2. *Fat:* include butter or margarine.
3. *Carbohydrate:* include sugar, bread and other sweet and starchy foods.
4. *Vitamins:*
     A: include milk, cheese, butter, margarine, green and yellow vegetables. Fish-liver oils for infants.
     B_1: include bread, yeast, meat.
     B_2: include milk, cheese and eggs.
     B_3: include bread, yeast, meat.
     C: include fresh fruit and vegetables, especially citrus fruit; orange juice for infants.
     D: include milk, butter, margarine.
5. *Minerals:*
     For iron, include meat, liver, bread, watercress.
     For calcium, include milk, cheese, bread.
     For iodine, include fish.
     For sodium, include salt.
     For other minerals, include fresh fruit and vegetables.
6. *Roughage:* include vegetables and fruits and wholemeal cereals.
7. *Water:* include plenty of drinks, soups, etc.

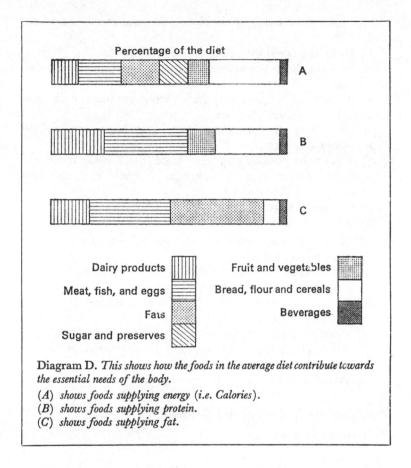

Diagram D. *This shows how the foods in the average diet contribute towards the essential needs of the body.*

(A) *shows foods supplying energy (i.e. Calories).*
(B) *shows foods supplying protein.*
(C) *shows foods supplying fat.*

The most important rules for meal planning are:

(*a*) Make sure that the diet contains enough protein, preferably some at each meal.

(*b*) Make sure it contains enough minerals and vitamins.

(*c*) Eat sweet and starchy foods mostly at the end of a meal to satisfy hunger.

(*d*) Have regular meal times and avoid eating between meals.

How to budget and shop

The following points must be considered carefully:

(*a*) Decide how much of the family income can be spent on food.

(*b*) Study the standard prices of the main foods.

(*c*) Plan meals for several days together, for economy of cost and time.

(*d*) Prepare a shopping list, which may be adapted to take advantage of genuine bargains.

(*e*) Shop where the shopkeeper pays attention to the hygiene of premises and assistants.

(*f*) Whenever possible buy in large quantities. Adequate storage for dry goods and root vegetables helps here, as also does a refrigerator and a freezer.

(*g*) Buy green vegetables and fruit as fresh as possible.

(*h*) When necessary to economize on food:

  (i) Select cheaper protein foods, e.g. cheese, milk, pulses, rather than meat.

  (ii) Select cheaper cuts of fish and meat, e.g. stewing meat rather than roasting joints.

  (iii) Use watercress or chopped cabbage as sources of vitamin C rather than fresh fruit.

  (iv) Cook using a method which is economical of fuel, e.g. cooking a whole meal at once in the oven, or in one steamer.

  (v) Avoid over-catering, and use up all left-over foods.

Planning Meals for Special Groups

Special meals for vegetarians

How	Why
1. Find out whether the food is for:	
(a) Strict vegetarians (vegans)	They eat nothing of animal origin; usually either for reasons of health or religion (though many will drink milk).
(b) Lacto vegetarians	They do not eat anything killed for food, e.g. meat, fish, or poultry, but they do eat eggs, cheese and milk dishes.

How	Why
2. Include adequate protein to replace meat, etc. for body-building.	For strict vegetarians use pulses, nuts and wholemeal cereals. For lacto vegetarians use dairy foods as well.
3. Season and flavour food well, using herbs, spices, etc.	To overcome the tastelessness of many vegetable foods.
4. Use vegetable fats or oils for cooking.	To avoid the use of animal fats such as lard and dripping.
5. Use vegetable extracts, e.g. Marmite, for flavouring gravies, etc.	To avoid the use of animal extracts.
6. Avoid too much carbohydrate.	Vegetarian diet tends to contain too much carbohydrate food.
7. Introduce variety and colour in the vegetables and serve them attractively.	To encourage appetite.
8. Serve some raw foods, e.g. fruits and salads.	To supply minerals and vitamins.
9. Use wholemeal cereals and wholemeal flour.	To supply more protein and minerals.
10. If digestion is poor give vegetables sieved as purées or as soups.	To avoid too much roughage.

Suitable dishes for vegetarians

Soups: Lentil, pea or vegetable purées, enriched with milk for lacto vegetarians.

Main meal dishes: Vegetable pie, pasty or flan. Vegetable stew, risotto or curried vegetables. Nut cutlets or substitute meat (from soya flour). Lacto vegetarians will also eat macaroni cheese, vegetables with cheese sauce, cheese pudding or soufflé, curried or stuffed eggs, omelettes.

Any of these dishes may be served with a selection of salads or cooked vegetables.

Breakfast dishes: Fresh fruit, cereals, porridge or muesli. Toast with marmalade, peanut butter or Marmite. For lacto vegetarians, any egg dish such as an omelette, boiled or scrambled egg.

Snacks and supper dishes: Vegetable tarts or pasties, salad sandwiches, mushrooms on toast, green salads with nuts. Lacto vegetarians will also eat egg or cheese salads, cheese flan or straws.

Sweets or puddings: Any fruit, fresh or cooked. Fruit, jam or nut pastries, avoiding the use of animal fats. Lacto vegetarians may be served with desserts made from milk, gelatine or eggs.

A typical day's menu for a lacto vegetarian
Breakfast: Grapefruit, scrambled egg on toast, wholemeal bread and butter, marmalade or honey, tea or coffee.
Dinner: Lentil soup, cheese and tomato flan, a green vegetable. Stewed fruit and custard.
Tea: Wholemeal scones and butter, fresh fruit and tea.
Supper: Salad with nuts or cheese, baked jacket potatoes. Baked egg custard and fruit. A milk or fruit drink before bedtime.

A typical day's menu for a strict vegetarian
Breakfast: Fresh orange juice, stewed prunes with cereal, toasted wholemeal bread with margarine and marmalade, or with peanut butter. Black coffee or cocoa, or lemon tea.
Dinner: Lentil soup, rice and corn salad with mixed raw vegetables (including watercress, chopped cabbage, shredded carrots, tomatoes and lettuce). Fresh fruit.
Tea: Wholemeal bread and Marmite, nuts and raisins, lemon tea.
Supper: Vegetable stew with jacket potatoes. Apricot tart with coconut cream. A fruit drink before bedtime.

Special meals for young children

How	Why
1. Supply children with a sufficient number of Calories.	To supply energy for rapid growth and physical activity.

How	Why
2. Give large amounts of body-building foods (proteins and minerals).	For growth of body tissue and bone.
3. Give plenty of the vitamin foods, fresh fruit, dairy foods, orange juice, cod liver oil.	Vitamin deficiency is serious in young children.
4. Give sweet foods at end of meal only, and avoid constant eating of sweets between meals.	To satisfy appetite only after essential nutrients have been supplied.
5. Give a large variety of foods.	To encourage children to eat different foods and to avoid faddiness.
6. Arrange for meals to be at regular times and in a happy atmosphere.	To encourage regular eating habits and to help digestion.
7. Include some crisp food, e.g. raw apple.	To exercise jaws and strengthen teeth.
8. Be sure that the child has at least 500 ml of milk each day.	To ensure the supply of essential nutrients.

A typical day's menu for a child under 5 years

Breakfast: Cereal or porridge, with milk and sugar. Egg, scrambled, boiled or poached. Bread and butter, milk and cod-liver oil.

Mid-morning: Orange juice.

Dinner: Stewed meat or steamed fish, mashed potatoes, a green vegetable, milk pudding with stewed fruit.

Tea: Sandwiches of watercress, or cheese and tomato. Wholemeal bread and butter, honey, a piece of cake.

Bedtime: Raw apple or carrot. Milk drink.

Special meals for invalids and convalescents

Obey the instructions of the doctor with regard to feeding, but the following rules will be found generally useful:

How	Why
1. Give plenty of body-building foods.	Loss of weight during illness must be made good.
2. Give plenty of fluids and vitamin foods.	To replace body fluid lost in illness, and to aid body repair.
3. Have suitable drinks always available.	Patient is often thirsty.
4. Make food attractive and as colourful as possible.	To tempt the appetite.
5. Be very particular about cleanliness in preparation and serving.	To avoid any further infection.
6. Choose foods which are light, nourishing and easily digested (steamed or grilled rather than fried).	Appetite and digestion are both poor after illness.
7. Give small meals at frequent intervals rather than large meals.	Patients will be encouraged to eat more.
8. Avoid all highly spiced or over-seasoned food.	Patients usually dislike strong flavours.
9. Avoid letting the smell of food during preparation reach the sickroom.	Invalids usually dislike the smell of cooking.

N.B. Milk drinks may be reinforced with eggs or patent foods. Fruit drinks may be sweetened with glucose. Lightly boiled eggs, egg custards, creamed fish or chicken and cream soups are all digestible and nourishing.

A typical day's menu for a convalescent patient who has had influenza
   Breakfast: Fresh fruit juice, lightly boiled egg, thin bread and butter, marmalade, weak tea or coffee.
   Mid-morning: A milk drink and a biscuit.
   Dinner: Baked white fish and parsley sauce, creamed potatoes and grilled tomatoes. Milk pudding or a light sponge pudding.

Tea: Wholemeal bread and butter, honey, Marmite or tomato sandwich; tea to drink.

Supper: Creamed soup, steamed lamb chop, mashed carrot or sieved green vegetable. Egg custard, fresh fruit.

Bedtime: A milk drink.

Special packed meals for picnics, or when a cooked meal is not obtainable

How	Why
1. Try to plan a well-balanced meal and to include some protein and vitamin foods.	It is easy to include too much carbohydrate as bread and pastry.
2. Avoid having food too dry, e.g. have moist fillings for sandwiches.	It is difficult to eat any food very dry.
3. Include drink, preferably carried in a vacuum flask.	It can be kept hot or cold.
4. Prepare food easy to pack.	
5. Pack food carefully, using containers, polythene bags, etc.	For cleanliness and convenience.

Suggestions for packed meals

1. Sandwiches: of cheese, meat, ham or eggs. Pasties containing meat, fish, cheese and vegetables. Small pork pies or sausage rolls. Crisp-bread biscuits with cream cheese and watercress. Small cottage pie packed in the vessel in which it was cooked. Any salad vegetables, packed in a plastic container.

2. Biscuits or shortbread, or any non-crumbly cake. Fruit turnovers, mince pies or jam tarts. Fresh fruit. A bar of chocolate. Nuts.

3. Tea, coffee or hot soup in a vacuum flask. Fruit drink in a bottle. Cold milk in a bottle.

Hints on making sandwiches

N.B. For cutting bread use a really sharp knife.

1. Use a loaf at least one day old, or if obtainable use thinly sliced bread. (The usual sliced loaf is often too thickly cut.)

2. Cream the butter or the margarine before spreading. Warm it slightly if necessary.

3. Spread the fat evenly.

4. Be generous with the filling, which should be fairly moist and well seasoned.

5. Experiment with fillings, e.g. grated apple and sultanas, chutney mixed with protein fillings.

6. Press the sandwiches firmly, and if for invalids or for a special occasion, cut off the crusts very thinly.

7. Wrap immediately in waxed or greaseproof paper or in a polythene bag.

The planning of meals for festive occasions

How	Why
1. Take care to have balanced meals.	It is easy to serve too much carbohydrate and insufficient body-building and protective foods.
2. Give both sweet and savoury dishes, and vary the flavour, colour and texture.	To suit all tastes.
3. Pay special attention to lay-out and serving. Be skilful with decorations and garnishes.	This can emphasize the reason for the party, e.g. with a centre-piece of birthday cake.
4. Include drinks; preferably both hot and cold.	
5. For a buffet meal, choose food which can be easily eaten while standing.	

Suggestions for a children's birthday party

Choose simple familiar dishes and present them attractively.

Choose something from each of the following groups:

1. Birthday Cake (this may be a simple Victoria Sandwich appropriately iced), small iced cakes, jam tarts, shortbread, small biscuits, meringues, etc.

2. Small sausage rolls, cheese straws, cheese scones, savoury sandwiches.

3. Buttered buns, scones, bread and butter.

4. Jelly, ice-cream, blancmange, fruit salad.

5. Milk, milk shakes, fruit drinks or weak tea (according to age of children).

Suggestions for buffet parties: indoors

1. Sausage rolls, savoury pasties, small meat pies, savoury flans, cheese straws, cheese scones, vol-au-vent cases with savoury fillings. Savoury sandwiches, or small rolls with a savoury filling. Small cooked sausages on sticks. Salad cut small with a salad dressing. Cold chicken joints.

2. Small iced cakes, eclairs, meringues, vanilla slices, biscuits of all kinds.

3. Jellies, trifles, mousses, creams, fruit salad, ice-cream, etc.

4. Coffee, tea and cold fruit drinks.

Suggestions for parties: out of doors

1. Fried sausages, tomatoes and mushrooms, Hamburgers, 'Hot Dogs', potatoes baked in jackets, toasted sandwiches, 'cheese dreams'.

2. Doughnuts, gingerbread, small cakes, biscuits.

3. Soup, coffee, fruit drinks, Coca-Cola, etc.

Suggestions for tea and coffee parties, etc.

1. For tea parties, serve thin bread and butter (white and wholemeal), buttered scones (plain or cheese), filled sandwiches or bridge rolls, cakes, biscuits and tea.

2. For morning coffee parties, serve biscuits, buns or small cakes, and coffee, with hot milk served separately.

3. For TV parties, serve individual trays with hot soup or coffee, cold savoury dishes, e.g. cheese flan or scotch eggs with a salad, a cold sweet, e.g. fruit salad or trifle, and bread rolls or bread and butter.

Economy in Catering

The general rule is to try to buy the correct amount for the number of people to be catered for, and thus to avoid having left-over food.

Table showing approximate amounts needed for each person

1. MEAT

Chops, cutlets or sheep's kidney	One
Stewing meat	100 g
Meat with bone	150 g
Joint for roasting or boiling	100–150 g
(A joint needs to be at least a kilo in weight to be cooked satisfactorily. This will do for several meals.)	
Sausages	100 g
Cooked cold meat	75–100 g

2. FISH

Fillets	100 g
Cutlets, including weight of bone	150 g
Small whole fish, such as herring, mackerel	One

3. VEGETABLES

Potatoes – old	200 g
– new	150 g
Green vegetables	100–150 g
Carrots and other roots	100 g
French or runner beans	100 g
Garden peas in pods	100 g
Tomatoes	50–75 g
Dried peas or other pulses	25 g
Watercress	25 g

4. FRUIT

Stewing fruit	100 g
Dried fruit	40 g

5. SOUP	125–250 ml
6. CHEESE	40 g
7. MILK PUDDING	175 ml
8. PUDDINGS, steamed or boiled	
PASTRY for tarts, etc.	40 g flour
9. CUSTARDS	125 ml
10. SAUCES AND GRAVIES	60 ml

Left-over Food

It must be used as soon as possible.

A réchauffé dish is one made from previously cooked food.

How

Why

Points to consider

1. Cooked food must be on a clean dish, covered, and kept very cold.

   To prevent spoilage or contamination.

2. While still warm, fish must be boned and flaked, potatoes mashed and meat minced.

   It is easier to do this while warm.

3. Before being reheated, meat and fish must be well seasoned and flavoured.

   Re-cooked food is usually insipid.

4. It must be moistened with a good gravy or sauce.

   Re-cooked food is usually dry.

5. Some foods require a protective covering, e.g. egg and bread-crumbs on croquettes.

   To prevent further drying during cooking.

6. All ingredients must be precooked.

7. Food must be finely cut or minced.

   To reduce reheating time.

8. Food must be reheated thoroughly, but only for a short time.

   To destroy bacteria, but long reheating hardens all proteins.

9. Do not give reheated foods to infants or invalids.

   They are less digestible than freshly cooked foods.

10. Always serve with some protective foods, e.g. salads, fresh green vegetables or fruit.

    To provide the vitamins destroyed by reheating.

11. Never reheat any dish more than once.

    Nearly all flavour will be lost.

Suggestions for the use of left-over food
1. COLD MEAT Shepherd's pie, mince, rissoles, croquettes, meat pasties, curries, stuffed vegetables.

2. COLD FISH Fish and potato pie, Russian fish pie, fish pasties, fish cakes, fish salad, soufflés.

3. POTATOES Sauté potatoes, bubble and squeak, fish pie, shepherd's pie, potato salad.

4. FAT FROM MEAT Clarify and use for frying.

5. STALE CHEESE Grate and use in cheese pastry, cheese savouries, sauces and soups.

6. SOUR MILK Cottage cheese, scones, etc.

7. STALE BREAD White crumbs for stuffings, steamed puddings, cheese pudding, coating fish.
   Crusts may be baked slowly and either used as rusks or crushed and used as browned crumbs.

8. STALE CAKE Trifles, queen of puddings or refrigerator flans.

9. EGG YOLKS For coating, for biscuit making or when scrambled for sandwich fillings.

Economy in the use of fuel
1. Save oven fuel by:
   (*a*) Cooking whole meal in oven, e.g. stew in casserole, together with potatoes in jackets and baked fruit pie.
   (*b*) Cooking together the dishes for several meals, e.g. cakes, flan cases, casserole dishes.
2. Save fuel on the hot plate by:
   (*a*) Standing several saucepans on one plate or burner (a set of triangular pans is economical).
   (*b*) Using a three-tiered steamer for whole meal, e.g. for steak and kidney pudding, cauliflower, potatoes, and stewed fruit in covered dish, all at the same time.
   (*c*) Using a pressure cooker which greatly reduces cooking time.
   (*d*) Cooking potatoes in a steamer over boiling root vegetables.
3. Fuel can be saved in all cases by not having the gas or electricity higher than necessary, and by turning off the gas or electricity as soon as it is no longer needed.

Convenience Foods

These are foods which are completely or partly prepared by the manufacturer. They are therefore easy or 'convenient' to use.

Examples of convenience foods are tinned foods of all kinds, dried soups and vegetables, frozen vegetables and fish, frozen or chilled pastry, stock cubes.

Advantages
1. They save time in preparation.
2. They save labour.
3. They require very little skill in preparation and cooking.
4. The quality is consistent.
5. There is no waste.
6. Many can be kept in larder or refrigerator for an emergency.

Disadvantages
1. They are expensive – some excessively so compared with the fresh products.
2. They often lack the fresh taste of untreated foods.
3. Vitamins are often lost during manufacture.

The saving in time and effort must be considered against the extra cost of convenience foods.

Time Planning

Besides being able to choose, prepare and cook well balanced and attractive meals the cook must be able to serve them punctually.

How to do this requires thought and organization, e.g.:

A housewife needs to prepare a meal for herself, her husband and two school age children. It must be served at 12.45 pm to fit in with her husband's lunch hour and the children's school hours.

Menu chosen
Beef and tomato casserole, boiled potatoes, green vegetable.
Stewed fruit and baked egg custard.

Why this choice
1. The cost of the meal fits into the family budget. It is economical on fuel, as it is mainly cooked in the oven.
2. It is nutritionally well balanced and liked by the family.

3. The preparation time allows the housewife time for other work or leisure activity during the morning.

4. The menu is flexible and the main course can be reheated in the evening if the husband is unable to reach home at lunch time. Tinned or frozen peas can then replace the fresh green vegetable and the second course can be served cold.

Recipe for the casserole

500 g stewing steak	Cut meat into cubes, coat in sea-
2 level tblesp flour	soned flour. Peel and chop onions.
salt, pepper, mixed herbs	Brown meat and onions in dripping.
25 g dripping	Place all ingredients in covered
2 large onions	casserole in a slow oven until meat
small tin tomatoes	is tender. Taste for seasoning add-
stock cube dissolved in	ing more if necessary.
375 ml boiling water	

List of ingredients needed

From store	*To buy*
dripping	500 g stewing steak
flour	onions
mixed herbs	plums or other fruit in season
salt, pepper	potatoes
stock cube	cabbage.
egg	
tin of tomatoes	
milk	
sugar.	

Time required for dishes

Dish	Preparation time	Cooking time
Beef and tomato casserole	½ hour	2 hours
boiled potatoes	5–10 minutes	20 minutes
cabbage	5 minutes	10 minutes
stewed fruit	5–10 minutes	40 minutes (in oven)
egg custard	10 minutes	45 minutes
dishing up	5 minutes	

From this it is obvious that the dishes needing the longest cooking time must be prepared first. The work should begin at 10.15 am.

Time plan

10.15 am	Collect equipment and ingredients, prepare meat and onions, make stock, open tin of tomatoes.
10.30 am	Preheat oven 150°C (Mark 2). Place ingredients in casserole.
10.45 am	Put casserole in oven. Prepare egg custard. Wash up dishes.
11 am	Break for an hour until 12 noon.
12 noon	Stand custard dish in a dish of water (bain marie). Put custard into oven. Place fruit with a little water and sugar to taste into another casserole, cover and put in oven.
12.15 pm	Prepare potatoes and put to boil. Boil water for cabbage, and prepare cabbage.
12.30 pm	Put cabbage to boil in boiling salted water. Lay the table. Tidy kitchen. Dish vegetables as they are cooked.
12.45 pm	Serve the meal.

EIGHT

Cooking
*What it is and why we cook food – Methods of cooking –
The 'how' and 'why' of each method.*

Cooking may be defined as the heating of food to bring about both physical and chemical changes.

Why food is cooked
1. *To make it safe to consume*

Milk is sterilized or pasteurized to destroy organisms of disease and at the same time to reduce the number of milk-souring bacteria.

Pork should always be well cooked to destroy any cysts of tape-worm which may be present.

Drinking water should be boiled if not obtained from a reliable source and known to be pure.

2. *To make it easier to swallow and to digest*

Starch grains swell when heated, and burst their walls so that the digestive juices can more easily penetrate into them.

The cellulose fibres and cell walls of fruit and vegetables are softened.

The connective tissue around the muscle fibres of meat softens and is turned to gelatine.

3. *To make it more attractive and appetizing*

The appearance of a well browned cake is more attractive than that of the dough from which it is made.

The smell of cooking can stimulate the appetite.

4. *To introduce variety in the diet*

Food can be cooked in various ways, e.g. eggs can be scrambled, boiled, poached, etc.

Flavours can be combined together such as those of meat, vegetables, seasoning and herbs in savoury dishes.

5. *To preserve food for later use*

Fruit may be bottled or made into jam.

How heat is applied to food during cooking

   1. *In the oven*

     Food is cooked by heat received:

     (*a*) By radiation from hot inner surfaces of the oven.

     (*b*) By convection, i.e. circulation of heated air.

     (*c*) By conduction from the metal bars of the oven, from roasting tins or aluminium foil. The heat reaches the centre of a joint from its surface by conduction.

   2. *The grill or rotating spit*

     Food is cooked by radiant heat. The use of 'Infra-red' grills speeds up the time of cooking.

   3. *The boiling plate*

     (*a*) Solid metal electric plate: the heat passes by conduction, so pans making good contact are necessary.

     (*b*) Radiant hot plate: heat passes to the pan placed on it by conduction and radiation.

     (*c*) Gas burners: heat passes to the pan by radiation, conduction and convection.

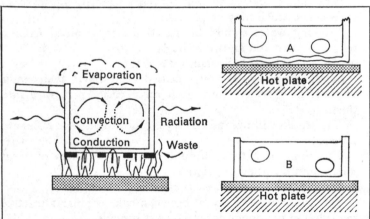

Fig. 10. Transference of heat during cooking. Heat passes through the pan to the liquid by conduction and is evenly distributed by convection currents. It passes from the outside to the inside of solid foods by conduction. Heat is also radiated from the outside of the pan.

    To avoid waste of heat remember: (1) Gas flame should not be allowed outside the base of pan. (2) Pans on hot plates should be placed to cover as much of the hot plate as possible. (3) Air is a very bad conductor of heat: an air film trapped as shown in (A) must not be permitted; the base of the pan must be in contact with the hot plate as in (B).

Saucepans

Heat applied to the pan is distributed through its liquid contents by convection currents, and to the centre of foods in the liquid by conduction.

Steamers

Steam condensing on the surface of food, or on a utensil containing it, releases latent heat which is absorbed by the food. Steam is at 100°C at normal atmospheric pressure.

Pressure cookers

Heat is similarly transferred but pressure can be built up in the pressure cooker, which is steam-tight, by adding weights. The increase in pressure causes the temperature inside the vessel to rise above normal boiling point so that cooking time is shortened.

Frying pans

Heat passes to and through food by conduction at a temperature of 180°C–250°C.

Methods of Cooking

'Dry' methods of cookery are baking, roasting, frying and grilling. 'Wet' methods of cookery are boiling, stewing and steaming. All these methods use water.
Braising is a combination of stewing and baking.

Grilling

Grilling is a dry method of cooking by means of heat radiated from a heated grill, or from a smokeless fire.

Foods suitable for grilling:

(*a*) Small, usually expensive cuts of meat, e.g. fillet or rump steak, lamb or pork chops and cutlets.

(*b*) Sausages, kidneys, liver, bacon rashers, etc.

(*c*) Whole small fish (e.g. herrings, mackerel) or fillets and cutlets of larger fish.

(*d*) Tomatoes, mushrooms.

Advantages: Food is quickly cooked, tasty, and there is no loss of soluble nutrients.

Disadvantages: Only suitable for the more tender and therefore more expensive cuts of meat. Needs considerable skill to do well.

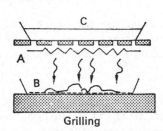

Grilling

Fig. 11. Grilling. Heat is radiated from the heated grill (A) on to the food in the grill pan (B). A pan or kettle containing water, (C) is put over the grill to reflect the heat downwards. This avoids wasting heat.

How	Why
1. Brush food with fat or oil unless it contains fat.	To prevent charring.
2. See that the grill is really hot before beginning to cook.	To seal the outside protein of the food and so prevent loss of juices.
3. Turn food frequently using tongs or two spoons (not forks).	To ensure that food is cooked evenly and to prevent loss of juices.
4. Serve quickly, without gravy, usually with chipped or sauté potatoes, tomatoes and mushrooms.	Food correctly grilled should be moist with its own juices.
5. Serve a suitable sauce, e.g. with steak serve maître d'hotel butter.	To add flavour and to increase food value.

Frying

Frying is the cooking of food in hot fat or oil usually between 180°C–205°C.

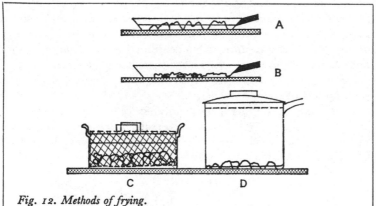

Fig. 12. Methods of frying.

(*A*) *Shallow frying with hot fat covering the bottom of the pan.*

(*B*) *Dry frying for fatty foods.*

(*C*) *Deep frying with enough fat to cover the food, with a removable wire basket.*

(*D*) *Sauté frying in a pan with the lid on, in a little fat.*

Fats suitable for frying should:

(*a*) be clean, and free from specks from previous frying which spoil the appearance of the food.

(*b*) be free from moisture, as the cooking temperature required cannot be reached until all the water is driven off.

(*c*) be free from any strong taste which might spoil the food.

(*d*) have a high decomposition temperature so that they do not burn easily.

They may be oils, e.g. olive, groundnut or corn oils, or soft fats, e.g. lard, cooking fats or clarified dripping. Butter may on occasion be used in shallow frying.

Foods suitable for frying:

(*a*) *For dry frying:* food containing fat, such as bacon, sausages, herrings. The fat melts and runs out of the food.

(*b*) *For sautéing:* foods which will absorb melted fat, such as potatoes, kidneys and vegetables for soup making.

(*c*) *For shallow frying:* foods which may be cooked in heated fat covering the bottom of the pan, e.g. eggs, cutlets, fish, pancakes, also batters.

(*d*) *For deep frying:* foods which can be cooked in sufficient fat to cover them, e.g. doughnuts, fish in batter.

Some foods require a coating before frying, such as seasoned flour or oatmeal, a batter of flour and milk, with or without egg, or egg and bread-crumbs. This coating prevents loss of flavour and nutrients and improves the appearance of the food.

Advantages of frying: Fried food is quickly cooked and tasty, with no loss of soluble nutrients.

Disadvantages: Frying is only suitable for the more expensive cuts of meat, needs skill and is dangerous unless done carefully – the fat may catch fire, particularly in deep fat frying. Fried food is not easily digested.

How	Why
1. Have fat absolutely clean.	Otherwise the appearance of the food is spoilt.
2. Have fat at correct temperature. When hot enough it should be still, without bubbles.	All the water has been driven off, but fat has not reached decomposition point.
3. Coat the outside of the food before deep frying.	To prevent the escape of juices and to prevent the food becoming soggy.
4. Do not fry too much food at once.	Temperature of fat is then lowered and food spoilt.
5. Turn food during shallow frying, and during deep frying if it floats, e.g. doughnuts. Turn the food carefully.	To ensure even cooking. To avoid scratching linings of pans.
6. Carefully drain fried food, if possible on kitchen paper.	To remove excess fat and to prevent food being soggy.

Roasting

Roasting really means cooking by radiated heat on a spit; it is also used to mean cooking in fat in the oven. This form of roasting is, of course, a type of baking.

Foods suitable for roasting:
   (*a*) Better cuts of meat, e.g. sirloin or rib of beef, leg of lamb or pork.
   (*b*) Poultry of all kinds if young.
   (*c*) Vegetables such as potatoes and parsnips, which can be cooked in the fat in the tin with the meat.
   Advantages: Appearance of food is usually good. Food is tasty and retains its full flavour and food value.
   Disadvantages: Needs attention and basting, or the food will be dry and hard. Only the tender and therefore expensive cuts of meat are suitable.

How	Why
1. Weigh and wipe the meat.	To be able to calculate the cooking time and to clean the meat.
2. Dust with seasoned flour.	To make a crisp tasty outside to the joint.
3. Have ready a large tin containing previously heated fat (lard or dripping). The tin may be covered or open. Place the meat in tin.	To develop the flavour of meat, and prevent loss of nutrients. The hot fat ensures a crisp outside coating.
4. EITHER put into hot oven at about 230°C (Mark 8) for 20 minutes and then reduce heat for rest of time.	To seal the outside protein.
OR place in a moderate oven at about 150°C (Mark 2) and cook slowly for about twice as long, OR cook from cold in modern quick-heating ovens.	To cook slowly and thus to soften the fibres if meat tends to be tough.

How	Why
5. If uncovered, baste frequently.	To keep meat moist and to prevent shrinkage.
6. Dish up when cooked and serve with gravy made from the meat juices left in the pan after pouring off the fat.	To avoid waste of flavour and of nutrients.

Cooking times for roasting in a hot oven
Beef: allow 15 minutes per 500 g and 15 minutes extra.
Lamb: allow 20 minutes per 500 g and 20 minutes extra.
Pork: allow 25 minutes per 500 g and 25 minutes extra.
Chicken: allow 20 minutes per 500 g and 20 minutes extra.

Baking

Baking is a dry method of cookery in which food is cooked in an oven which may be pre-heated to the required temperature, usually between 95°C and 260°C (Marks $\frac{1}{4}$–9).

Foods suitable for baking:
(*a*) Meat (see Roasting).
(*b*) Whole fish or large cutlets.
(*c*) Vegetables, e.g. potatoes, onions (not green vegetables).
(*d*) Pastry, Cakes, Yeast Mixtures, etc.
Advantages: There is no loss of soluble nutrients. Food does not break up, but keeps its shape. Food has an attractive appearance.
Disadvantages: Requires attention, otherwise food may burn. It is expensive to heat the oven, and therefore wasteful to bake only one dish.

Baking of flour mixtures
The rules vary with different mixtures and these will be dealt with in Chapter 10.

Baking of fish

How	Why
1. Prepare and wash fish. Stuff if desired.	To clean it and to add extra flavour.
2. Place in greased dish, cover with small dabs of fat, season, and cover with greased paper.	To keep fish moist during cooking.
3. Bake at about 180°C (Mark 4) for approximately 10 minutes per 500 g.	

Baking of vegetables

How	Why
1. Wash well. Cook in skins if possible.	To avoid loss of food value.
2. Prick skins of potatoes.	To prevent bursting due to generation of steam.
Do not prick beetroot.	To prevent loss of colour.
3. Cook in moderate oven until tender.	

Boiling

Boiling is a method of cooking carried out in liquid at a temperature of 100°C. In practice it is usually done in a covered pan. Large joints of meat, etc. are usually brought to the boil, and then allowed to simmer at a slightly lower temperature.

Foods suitable for boiling:
   (a) Large joints of medium quality meat, either fresh or salted, e.g. silverside, brisket, ox tongue, ham.
   (b) Large fish, e.g. salmon, cod, hake.
   (c) All vegetables and pulses.
   (d) Four mixtures, e.g. dumplings.
   (e) Soups, stocks.

Advantages: Simple and requires little attention. Economical of fuel, as a whole course may be cooked in the same pan, meat and vegetable together. Boiling is a moist method and therefore softens tough cuts of meat.

Disadvantages: Loss of soluble nutrients in the water: food often looks unattractive: food may break into pieces during cooking: it is a rather long, slow method.

How	Why
1. Soak salted or dried foods.	To remove excess salt and to replace water lost during dehydration.
2. Have a large pan with sufficient water to cover the food. Heat to boiling point. Add salt if needed.	Food cooks even if completely covered.
3. Put in food and boil for 5 minutes.	To seal the outside of meat and thus retain the juices.
4. Reduce temperature slightly and simmer until tender.	To avoid breaking food into pieces.
5. Whenever possible, use the cooking water for soups, gravy or sauces.	To make use of the soluble nutrients.
6. Serve with suitable sauces and garnishes.	To improve the rather dull appearance.

NOTE. Vegetables, especially green vegetables, are NOT boiled in large quantities of water, but in just enough to prevent burning (the conservative method – see Chapter 5).

Steaming

Steaming is a moist method of cooking by steam from boiling liquid. Steaming may be either by direct contact between the food and the steam, as in a steamer, or by indirect contact when the steam reaches only the container, as when the food is in a covered basin or between two plates.

Foods suitable for steaming:

(*a*) Small pieces of meat, e.g. chops, cutlets, liver.
(*b*) Small fish or fillets, e.g. whiting, cod steaks.
(*c*) Root vegetables and potatoes, but not green vegetables.
(*d*) Fresh and dried fruit.
(*e*) Puddings, suet pastry, batter mixtures, egg custards.

Advantages: No loss of nutrients, or flavour: no fat is added, so the food remains light and easily digested and therefore suitable for infants and invalids: economical of fuel, as the whole meal can be cooked on one burner: needs little attention except to see that the water does not boil away or come off the boil. Food remains whole and is not broken up.

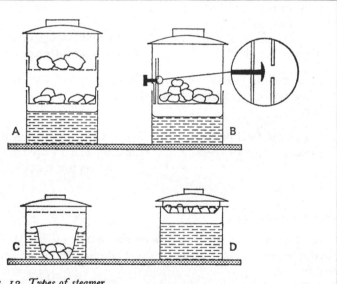

Fig. 13. Types of steamer.
(*A*) *Tiered steamer. Each tier has a perforated base and the bottom one fits on to a pan of boiling water.*
(*B*) *Tiered steamer. Each tier has a solid base but is fitted with a tube up which steam passes into the next tier through a hole controlled by a movable knob. (One tier only is shown.)*
(*C*) *Covered basin standing in a pan of boiling water.*
(*D*) *Plate covered with a lid, standing over a pan of boiling water.*

Disadvantages: It is a lengthy process. Dishes are sometimes unattractive in appearance unless skill is used in dishing up. Sauces and garnishes are required.

How	Why
1. Food should be steamed either:	
in a steamer,	
or in a covered basin standing in boiling water,	
or between two plates over a pan of boiling water.	
The lid of the steamer must always fit tightly.	To prevent loss of steam and to keep temperature constant.
2. Add boiling water to pan when necessary during cooking.	To keep up a constant supply of steam.
3. Cover the food or wrap it in greased paper or metal foil.	To prevent loss of juices during cooking, and to prevent foods from becoming sodden.

Pressure Cooking

It must be stressed that it is very important indeed to follow exactly the instructions given by the manufacturer of the pressure cooker.

Pressure cooking is cooking by superheated steam in a closed vessel with a strong and firmly secured lid and safety valve. As the steam cannot easily escape, the pressure is increased inside the cooker, and the liquid boils at a higher temperature. With many makes of pressure cooker the pressure is increased by adding a series of valve weights. The higher the pressure, the greater the temperature and the shorter the cooking time. The corresponding rise of temperature with pressure is as follows:

pressure	*temperature*
atmospheric pressure	boiling point 100°C
L (lowest weight representing about 2·25 kg)	108·5°C
M (medium weight representing about 4·5 kg)	115·3°C
H (highest weight representing about 7 kg)	112°C

Advantages: Very quick method: tough coarse foods can be softened easily and quickly: very economical of fuel: no loss of nutrients.

Disadvantages: Needs skill and experience. There is danger from careless handling of pressure cookers.

How	Why
1. Put a small amount of water into the cooker.	Very little is needed, as steam does not escape.
2. Put in food. Do not over-crowd cooker.	This allows room for steam.
3. Put on lid with valve open and heat for a few minutes.	To drive out the air.
4. Close valve and heat until valve hisses, or until dial shows correct pressure.	To build up the pressure.
5. Reduce the heat and start timing the cooking.	Required pressure and temperature are reached.
6. After given time, cool the cooker. Then carefully open the valve and then open the cooker.	This reduces pressure inside cooker to that of the atmosphere.

Stewing

Stewing is a long slow method of cooking food in a small quantity of liquid, at a temperature just below boiling point, about 82°C. This can be carried out in a tightly covered pan on top of the cooker, or in a covered casserole in the oven. The liquid is at simmering point.

Foods suitable for stewing:
    (*a*) Fresh and dried fruits.
    (*b*) All vegetables except green ones.
    (*c*) Cheaper, coarser cuts of meat, e.g. shin of beef, scrag end or breast of lamb.

Advantages: Makes appetizing and attractive dishes from cheaper cuts of meat and vegetables: economical of fuel, as only a small amount of heat is required: requires little attention during cooking: no loss of nutrients as the liquid is served with the food.

Disadvantages: Takes a long time.

How	Why
1. Cut food into small pieces.	To expose maximum surface area to heat.
2. Add sufficient liquid barely to cover food.	To get maximum flavour in the cooking liquid.
3. Make sure the temperature is just below boiling point.	To prevent the food breaking up, meat becoming stringy, and fruit pulping.
4. For a brown stew lightly fry meat and vegetables first.	To improve colour and flavour.

Braising

Braising is a method of cookery which combines stewing and baking. It is suitable for medium quality cuts of meat and for vegetables.

The food is cooked until tender in a covered pan with a little fat and a little seasoned liquid, and is then browned in the oven, after the lid has been removed.

NINE

Raising Agents
*Air, yeast and chemical mixtures – What they are – How
they are used – How and why they work.*

Raising agents are substances added to mixtures in order to make
them lighter and more open in texture, and therefore more pleasant to eat and easier to digest. Raising agents are either gases, e.g.
air, or substances from which gases are produced, e.g. yeast,
baking powder and bicarbonate of soda.

How raising agents work
   1. The raising agent provides bubbles of gas in the mixture
(air, beaten or folded in, or carbon dioxide produced from yeast,
baking powder or bicarbonate of soda). Bubbles of steam will be
produced from the water and water vapour in a mixture when it is
heated.
   2. These bubbles of gas and vapour expand when heated.
   3. The protein of flour mixtures (gluten) is elastic and is
stretched by the expanding gases.
   4. The heat during cooking 'sets' the gluten and so forms the
rigid framework of the flour product.

Classification of raising agents
   1. *Air:* this can be introduced into a mixture by:
   (*a*) Sieving the flour (the air is trapped between the grains).
   (*b*) Raising the flour above the bowl when rubbing in fat.
   (*c*) Beating the mixture as for batters.
   (*d*) Creaming fat and sugar as in rich cake-making.
   (*e*) Whisking eggs (either whole or whites only).
   (*f*) Folding between layers as in flaky pastry.
   The amount of air included cannot be accurately measured but
is judged by the appearance of the mixture, e.g. a whisked sponge
cake should be thick and creamy.
   2. *Yeast:* This is a mass of living micro-organisms which in
order to grow and to produce carbon dioxide need food and

TABLE SHOWING USE OF RAISING AGENTS

	AIR	YEAST	CHEMICAL RAISING AGENTS
Nature	Mixture of gases	Living Cells	Sodium bicarbonate used alone or with an acid
Method of adding to mixture	Beating Whisking Sieving flour Creaming Folding pastry, etc.	Mixed with sugar or liquid, or rubbed into flour	Sieved with flour
Amount used with 500 g flour	Not measurable – judged by appearance	15 g (for up to 500 g) (25 g for ½–1½ kg) (50 g for 1½–3½ kg)	2 teasp. baking powder 1 teasp. bicarbonate or 1 teasp. bicarbonate and 2 teasp. cream of tartar
Effect of using too much	No effect	Coarse texture Sour taste Loaf may collapse	Mixture rises too rapidly and sinks in the middle Too much bicarbonate gives a sour taste
Points to remember in use	Mixture may stand before cooking. No escape of air occurs	Yeast works more quickly if warm, but quite satisfactorily in the cold. It is destroyed by over heating	Mixture should be baked immediately as some carbon dioxide is given off as soon as mixture is moistened
Examples of use	Pastries Whisked sponge Batters	Bread Buns	Gingerbread Scones Plain cake mixtures

moisture (see bread making). It can be introduced into a mixture by adding it to sugar or liquid and then adding the result to the flour, or by rubbing it into the flour. It is distributed evenly by kneading the dough.

3. *Chemical raising agents*

(*a*) *Sodium bicarbonate*, used alone as in gingerbread. This can be added with the flour. When liquid is added and the mixture is heated, the bicarbonate decomposes and forms carbon dioxide, water and sodium carbonate. The latter substance can give a slightly unpleasant taste, but this is masked by the strong flavour of the ginger.

(*b*) *Sodium bicarbonate used with an acid substance*, e.g. sour milk as in scones.

The sodium bicarbonate reacts with the lactic acid in the milk forming carbon dioxide, sodium lactate and water.

(*c*) *Baking powder* is a mixture of 1 part sodium bicarbonate with 2 parts of cream of tartar (or 1 part tartaric acid). Starch in some form, or lactose, is usually added to absorb any moisture and thus improve the keeping quality of the powder, and also to slow down the reaction.

When water is added the sodium bicarbonate reacts with the cream of tartar forming carbon dioxide, water and sodium potassium tartrate. This is a tasteless substance known as Rochelle Salt.

TEN

Mixtures Using Flour
Pastry, cakes, batters, biscuits, scones and yeast mixtures.

Pastry Making

Pastry is a mixture of flour, salt, fat and water. The variety and texture of the pastry depends on the proportions of these ingredients, on the way in which they are incorporated, and on the method of cooking.

Ingredients used

1. *Flour:* Use plain flour, preferably a 'weak' one for shortcrust and suet pastries, and a 'strong' one for flaky and puff pastries.

2. *Baking powder:* Use only in suet pastry (or in short crust pastry if it is necessary to use less than half fat to flour).

3. *Salt:* Use 1 teaspoonful to each 500 g of flour to improve the flavour and to strengthen the gluten.

4. *Water:* Use as cold as possible, and just enough to obtain the desired consistency.

5. *Lemon juice:* This may be added to the richer pastries to counteract the richness and to make the gluten more elastic.

6. *Fat:* Use the type and quantity required by the recipe, which will also determine the method of adding the fat. Suet, butter, cooking fat, margarine, lard or a mixture of margarine and lard, or margarine and butter, may be used, according to the type of pastry.

Aims in pastry making

1. *Lightness:* This depends on the amount of raising agent. In most pastries, this raising agent is AIR, which expands when heated. Baking powder is used in suet pastry as suet melts slowly, and the starch grains in the flour may harden before absorbing the fat. This pastry is best cooked by steaming or boiling as baking hardens it.

2. *Shortness:* Short pastry should crumble easily. This is achieved

by rubbing in fat without oiling, by using only just enough water to bind it together, by light handling and by baking in a hot oven.

3. *Flakiness:* in rough puff, flaky and puff pastries. This is achieved by ̊olding in the maximum amount of air, by careful rolling and by baking at the correct oven temperature.

General rules for pastry making
1. Use good quality PLAIN flour.
2. Keep everything as cool as possible.
3. Introduce as much air as possible during the making.
4. Allow pastries (except suet) to relax after making, before cooking.
5. Roll lightly with short quick forward strokes.
6. Bake at the correct oven temperature – the richer the pastry, the hotter the oven. (See table on page 106.)

Principles underlying the making and cooking of pastry
1. Air incorporated during the making expands during the cooking.
2. The expanding air stretches the elastic gluten of the flour.
3. The fat melts.
4. The starch grains in the flour swell and burst in the heat and absorb the fat and some water.
5. The gluten coagulates and sets the 'framework' of the pastry.
6. Surplus water evaporates.
7. The starch grains on the surface are turned to dextrin in baking, thus giving a brown colour to the pastry.
NOTE. A hot oven must be used, otherwise the fat will melt before the starch grains burst, and the fat will run out.

The most common types of pastry:

How	Why
SUET	
1. Sieve 250 g flour with 1 rounded teaspoon baking powder and 1 level teaspoon salt.	To aerate the flour. Baking powder to provide extra raising agent. Salt to improve flavour.
2. Add 75 g suet finely chopped or shredded and mix.	To distribute it evenly in the mixture.

How	Why
3. Add about 125 ml cold water to make a soft but not sticky dough. Knead lightly with finger tips.	To make a smooth, even dough.
4. Roll to required shape.	
5. Cook by steaming.	Suet melts slowly – a slow moist method is best.

How	Why
SHORT	
1. Sieve 250 g plain flour with 1 level teaspoon salt.	To aerate the flour and to improve the flavour.
2. Add 125 g fat (butter, margarine, lard or a mixture).	
3. Rub fat into flour with tips of fingers, including as much air possible.	To keep the mixture as cool as possible and to aerate it.
4. Add about 50 ml very cold water and mix to a stiff dough.	Too much water makes a tough pastry.
5. Knead lightly.	To make an even dough.
6. Roll once only into shape required. Roll lightly.	To avoid stretching the pastry.
7. Set the dough aside in a cool place to relax.	To avoid shrinkage in cooking.
8. Cook in a hot oven.	To cause rapid expansion of air, bursting of the starch grains and absorption of the fat.

How	Why

ROUGH PUFF

1. Sieve 250 g flour and 1 level teaspoon salt.

To aerate the flour.

2. Cream 150 g fat and cut into about twelve lumps. Use butter, margarine, lard or a mixture.

Fat should be of the same consistency as the dough.

3. Toss the fat in the flour.

To separate the lumps.

4. Add 125 ml cold water and ¼ teaspoon lemon juice to make a soft dough.

To counteract richness.

5. Mix with a palette knife.

To avoid breaking the fat.

6. Shape into a rectangle and roll lightly into a long strip.

7. Fold neatly into three, enclosing as much air as possible. Close and seal ends.

To separate each layer of pastry with air.

8. Give pastry a half turn and repeat the rolling and folding twice more.

To give several layers to the pastry.

9. Set it aside to relax.

To avoid shrinkage during cooking.

10. Roll into shape required.

11. Bake in a very hot oven.

To cause rapid expansion of air and to burst the starch grains and so enable them to absorb the fat as it melts.

How	Why

FLAKY

1. Sieve 250 g flour and 1 level teaspoon salt.

To aerate the flour.

2. Cream 175 g of fat (a mixture of margarine and lard).

To make the fat the same consistency as the dough.

How	Why

3. Rub ¼ of the fat into the flour and mix to a soft dough with 125 ml cold water and ¼ teaspoon lemon juice. — A soft dough is easy to roll and of the same consistency as the fat.

4. Knead lightly. — To develop gluten. To make a smooth dough.

5. Roll into an even oblong strip and put another ¼ of the fat in small lumps on to ⅔ of the dough. — To ensure even distribution of the fat.

6. Fold evenly to produce alternate layers of dough and fat; seal the edges with the rolling pin. — To enclose as much air as possible and to produce the flaky layers.

7. Give pastry a half turn and repeat the rolling and addition of fat twice more.

8. Allow pastry to relax in a cool place. — To avoid shrinkage during cooking.

9. Roll and fold twice more. — To make pastry really flaky.

10. Bake in a very hot oven for 15–20 minutes. — To expand the air and thus to separate the layers.

11. Reduce the oven temperature slightly. — To cook thoroughly without burning.

Alternative method:
1. Make dough without any fat.
2. Knead very well as for bread.
3. Roll out and put ⅓ of the fat on ⅔ of the pastry.

Continue as in other recipe.

TABLE COMPARING THE MOST COMMON PASTRIES

	SUET	SHORT	ROUGH PUFF	FLAKY
Flour	Plain with baking powder or self-raising	Plain	Plain	Plain
Type of Fat	Suet	Butter, margarine, lard or cooking fat	Mixture of butter or margarine and lard	Mixture of butter or margarine and lard
Proportion of Fat to Flour	$\frac{1}{3}$	$\frac{1}{2}$	$\frac{2}{3}$	$\frac{3}{4}$
Raising Agent	Baking powder	Air	Air	Air
Consistency	Soft	Stiff	Soft	Soft
Method of Cooking	Steaming, boiling or baking in a moderate oven	Baking in a hot oven or frying	Baking in a very hot oven	Baking in a very hot oven
Uses	Steamed puddings, dumplings, jam roly-poly etc.	Fruit pies, pasties, tarts, flans, meat pies using pre-cooked meat	Meat pies, sausage rolls, mince pies, eccles cakes, etc.	As for Rough Puff

Why failures sometimes happen in pastry making

Failures may be due to any of the following reasons:

1. Insufficient air has been incorporated, or not enough baking powder used in suet pastry.

2. Too much liquid, causing a hard and tough pastry.

3. Too much handling in rolling out, causing a hard, badly risen pastry.

4. No time allowed for relaxing of pastry, which then shrinks on cooking.

5. Too cool an oven, causing an ill-risen greasy pastry.

6. Too hot an oven, causing pastry to be hard on the outside and soggy inside.

Cake Making

Cakes are made from a mixture of flour, sugar, and usually fat, eggs and a liquid. They vary in taste and texture according to the proportions of the ingredients used, and the method of preparation and of cooking.

Ingredients used in cake making

1. *Flour:* Use a 'weak' or 'soft' flour, i.e. one with a high starch and low gluten content. This gives cakes a good even texture. For plain cake mixtures self-raising flour may be used, but for rich mixtures plain flour is better, as the amount of baking powder needed depends on the type of mixture and the amount of air included.

2. *Sugar:* Use caster sugar, unless otherwise specified in the recipe, as it dissolves easily and creams readily with fat. Soft brown sugar may be used in fruit cakes and gingerbread, to give a dark colour. Sugar sweetens the mixture, helps to brown the outside of the cake as it caramelizes during baking, and makes the gluten framework soft in texture.

3. *Fat:* Butter gives the best flavour but margarine is a good substitute. Both cream easily with sugar. Cooking fats cream easily but have very little flavour. Lard and dripping have characteristic tastes which in some mixtures can be disguised with spices. Fats are used to give a soft texture and a good flavour, and to improve the keeping quality of the mixture.

A PLAIN cake is one with less than half fat to flour. A RICH cake is one with half or more fat to flour.

Fat may be added to cake mixtures in one of three methods:

(*a*) Rubbing into the flour with the fingertips.

(*b*) Creaming with the sugar.

(*c*) Melting, usually with sugar or treacle, and adding to the dry ingredients.

4. *Eggs:* When beaten, eggs have the property of entangling air, which acts as a raising agent. The protein of eggs together with the gluten of the flour forms the framework of the cooked cake. Eggs also give flavour and colour, and the fat in the yolk enriches the mixture.

5. *Liquids:* The liquids used are milk, water or eggs, and the amount depends on the required consistency of the mixture. Milk increases the food value and improves the flavour. Eggs do both these things and also help in the raising. Liquids are necessary to bind the mixture, to make the gluten elastic, to dissolve soluble constituents such as sugar, to enable baking powder to produce carbon dioxide, and to provide steam which helps to raise the cake.

6. *Raising agents:* Air is the main raising agent and is added to mixtures by:

(*a*) Rubbing fat into flour.

(*b*) Creaming fat and sugar.

(*c*) Whisking eggs alone or with sugar.

Baking powder is used in plain cake mixtures (or self-raising flour may be used). Bicarbonate of soda is used in ginger-bread mixtures as it helps to make them dark in colour, and the spices disguise the taste of the sodium carbonate left in the mixture.

Aims in cake making

1. Even 'open' texture which depends on the correct proportion of ingredients and on correct mixing and cooking.

2. Good and even rising which depends on the correct amount of raising agent and on correct baking.

3. Attractive appearance, which depends on correct baking.

4. Pleasant flavour, which depends on using good quality ingredients in the correct proportions.

General rules for cake making

1. Prepare the tin: For plain and whisked mixtures grease lightly.

For rich and melted fat mixtures line the tin with **greaseproof paper**.

2. Weigh or measure the ingredients accurately.

3. In mixing:

(*a*) Mix dry ingredients thoroughly.

(*b*) Blend fat in carefully.

(*c*) Fold in flour very lightly.

(*d*) Dry any fruit well before adding to mixture.

(*e*) Mix to the correct consistency according to the recipe.

4. Bake mixture at the correct heat for the particular cake as given in the recipe. In general:

(*a*) The richer the cake the slower the oven.

(*b*) The larger the cake the slower the oven.

5. Test when done. Cake should be:

(*a*) Springy to the touch.

(*b*) Well risen and brown.

(*c*) Shrinking from the sides of the tin.

6. Cool well on a wire rack, and store in an airtight tin.

Principles underlying the methods of cake making

1. *By the rubbing-in method:* rubbing-in evenly distributes the fat in the mixture. When liquid is added, the bicarbonate of soda and cream of tartar react to give off carbon dioxide.

2. *By the creaming method:* when fat and sugar are creamed together air is entrapped and the ingredients are evenly mixed. Flour is later folded in carefully. If flour is beaten in, this will knock the air out of the mixture.

3. *By the whisking method:* whisked egg and sugar entangle air. The flour is again folded in carefully, and not beaten.

4. *By the melted fat method:* melted fat is added with the liquid, since this ensures even distribution. Bicarbonate of soda is the usual raising agent. This substance, when heated, gives off carbondioxide.

In all cakes the following changes occur:

When put into the oven the mixture becomes hot, and the gases in the mixture (carbon dioxide and air) and the water vapour produced from the liquids expand, stretching the elastic gluten of the flour, and so making the cake rise. The gluten and the egg albumen 'set' with the heat of the oven to form the framework of the cake. The heat also causes the starch cells in the flour to burst their walls, and the fat to melt. The fat and other liquids are absorbed by the starch grains, and some of the water evaporates. On the outside the starch is turned to dextrin and the sugar to caramel, giving the brown colour to the finished cake.

Why cakes are sometimes failures

This may be due to:

1. Too much or too little raising agent.
2. Wrong proportion of other ingredients.
3. Too much or too little liquid and therefore wrong consistency.
4. Not whisking or creaming enough or too vigorous beating or folding in of flour.
5. Too hot or too cold an oven.

Methods of cake making

I. MELTED FAT METHOD

How	Why
1. Sieve 250 g flour with all dry ingredients.	To aerate flour and to mix thoroughly.
2. Heat 75 g fat, 75 g sugar and 100 g syrup. Let fat melt but do not overcook.	To avoid changes in the sugar caused by overheating.
3. Add mixture to flour, etc. together with enough liquid to make thick batter.	To blend thoroughly and to start action of raising agent.
4. Mix gently with metal spoon but do not beat.	To avoid a tough texture.

How	Why
5. Pour into a greased and lined tin.	To prevent burning.
6. Bake in a slow oven (150°C, Mark 2) until well risen and firm.	Carbon dioxide is produced slowly from bicarbonate of soda.
7. Keep for 24 hours before eating.	Mixture improves with keeping, centre becomes soft, and the outside sticky.

2. RUBBING IN METHOD

How	Why
1. Sieve 200 g flour, pinch of salt and 1 level teaspoon baking powder.	To aerate the mixture.
2. Rub 75–100 g fat in with finger tips.	To distribute evenly.
3. Add 75–100 g sugar, flavourings and mix with beaten egg and milk to make soft, dropping consistency.	To blend thoroughly and to start action of baking powder.
4. Put into greased cake tin.	To prevent sticking.
5. Bake large cake in a moderate oven (180°C, Mark 4) and small cakes in hot oven (200°C, Mark 6).	To allow the carbon dioxide to expand before the gluten sets framework of cake.
6. Store in an airtight tin but use within three days.	To stop the cakes from going dry because the proportion of fat is low.

3. CREAMING METHOD

How	Why
1. Beat 100 g fat and 100 g sugar with wooden spoon until light creamy.	To enclose air and to break down sugar crystals.
2. Beat 2 eggs until light and fluffy.	To enclose air.
3. Add eggs gradually, beating well.	To prevent 'curdling', i.e. fat separating from sugar and eggs.
4. Sieve 150 g flour and ½ level teaspoon baking powder and fold in lightly with a metal spoon.	To add more air and to avoid knocking air out by beating in flour.
5. Put into a paper-lined tin. Greasing is not usually necessary.	To prevent burning. There is usually enough fat in mixture to prevent sticking.
6. Bake in a moderate oven (190°C, Mark 5) for small cakes (170°C, Mark 3) for large cakes.	To allow gases to expand before gluten sets.
7. Cool when cooked and store in airtight tin where the cakes can be kept for some time.	Because the high fat content keeps them moist.

3a. ALTERNATIVE AND QUICKER METHOD

How	Why
1. Put the same ingredients in the mixing bowl all together. Use a soft margarine, roughly cut, and unbeaten eggs.	This saves time in preparation.

How	Why
2. Add 2 tablespoonfuls of milk and an extra level teaspoon of baking powder.	The extra liquid makes the mixture easier to beat, and the extra raising agent replaces the air incorporated by the ordinary methods.
3. Beat for 1 minute with a wooden spoon.	
4. Bake as usual.	

4. WHISKING METHOD (WITH NO FAT)

How	Why
1. Whisk 2 eggs and 50 g sugar together until thick and creamy (easier over pan of hot water).	Sugar dissolves and air is held by the mixture.
2. Sieve 50 g flour and a pinch of baking powder evenly over mixture.	To separate the flour grains.
3. Fold flour in carefully with a metal spoon.	To avoid knocking out air.
4. Pour into tins, greased and sprinkled with caster sugar and flour.	This gives a sweet crusty outside to the cake.
5. Bake immediately in a moderate oven (180°C, Mark 4) until set. Do not open oven door too soon.	Mixture easily sinks if cooled by air before it is set.
6. Turn on to a wire tray and cool away from draughts.	To ensure even cooling.
7. Do not store long before use.	As they contain no fat, they dry quickly.

TABLE COMPARING METHODS OF CAKE MAKING

	MELTED FAT METHOD	RUBBING-IN METHOD	CREAMING METHOD	WHISKING METHOD
Proportion of ingredients	⅓ fat to flour ⅓ sugar to flour ¾ treacle or syrup to flour 1 egg to 250 g flour (optional) Enough milk	⅓–½ fat to flour ⅓–½ sugar to flour 1 egg to 200 g flour Enough milk	½–1 fat to flour ½–1 sugar to flour 2–4 eggs to 200 g flour Enough milk	No fat 50 g sugar, 50 g flour, to every egg used Usually no extra liquid
Consistency	To make Thick batter	To make Soft dropping	To make Dropping	Thick and creamy

Flour and Raising Agent	S.R. flour + ½ level teaspoon bicarbonate of soda to 250 g flour	S.R. flour or plain flour + 2 level teaspoons baking powder to 200 g flour	Plain flour with amount of baking powder decreasing with richness	S.R. flour
Fat and Method of Adding it	Lard, margarine or dripping melted with sugar and syrup, and added to dry ingredients	Margarine or butter, rubbed into flour with finger tips	Margarine or butter beaten with sugar until creamy	None
Oven Heats				
Large cakes:	150°C, Mark 2 – slow	180°C, Mark 4 – moderate	170°C, Mark 3 – slow	180°C, Mark 4 – moderate
Small cakes:	180°C, Mark 4 – moderate	200°C, Mark 6 – hot	190°C, Mark 5 – fairly hot	180°C, Mark 4 – moderate
Examples				
Large cakes:	Gingerbread Malt loaf	Plain fruit cake Coconut cake	Victoria sandwich Christmas cake	Sponge sandwich Swiss roll
Small cakes:	Gingerbuns Parkins	Rock cakes Jam buns	Queen cakes Cup cakes	Sponge cakes Sponge fingers

Batter Making

Batters are mixtures of flour, milk and generally eggs. They rise during cooking because the gases incorporated during the mixing expand. The water vapour produced from the liquid used is the most important raising agent. Air is put into the mixture by beating or whisking, and is retained by the beaten eggs. If no eggs are used, baking powder is usually added.

Types of Batters

1. *Plain coating batter*. This is used for coating foods before frying. 100 g flour is blended with 125 ml milk, and salt and baking powder added. This forms a thick coating batter.

2. *Egg batter*. Flour, salt, eggs and milk are blended and whisked to incorporate air. Use 100 g flour, 1 egg and 125 ml milk for a thick coating batter, and use 100 g flour, 1 egg and 250 ml milk for a thin batter for pancakes, Yorkshire puddings, toad-in-the-hole, batter puddings, etc.

Aims in batter making

1. Lightness: This depends on
(a) The amount of air which is incorporated into the mixture.
(b) The correct cooking temperature, i.e. high at first to cause rapid expansion of the gases, and later a lower temperature to ensure that the inside is cooked.

2. Crispness in baked or dried batters. This depends on the correct temperature of the oven or of frying fat (190°C, Mark 5). This will brown the outside and also cook the inside thoroughly without burning.

Principles of batter making

1. Air is beaten into the mixture. Egg albumen retains air.
2. Water vaporizes in heat of cooking.
3. Gases and water vapour expand on heating and stretch the elastic gluten in the mixture.
4. Albumen of egg and gluten of flour set in the heat.
5. Starch grains burst in the heat and absorb liquid.
6. Starch on the outside is turned to dextrin.

Method of making a basic egg batter

How	Why
1. Sieve 100 g flour and 1 level teaspoon salt.	To mix and aerate.
2. Make a hollow in centre of flour, add 1 egg. Stir well.	To blend ingredients smoothly.
3. Add 125 ml milk to make a creamy consistency. Beat or whisk thoroughly.	To incorporate as much air as possible.
4. Add a further 125 ml of milk. Stir.	Difficult to beat if batter is very liquid.
5. Baking: Pour into hot well-greased tin. Bake in hot oven (200°C, Mark 6). Frying: Fry in hot fat. Steaming: Pour into greased basin. Cover and steam over boiling water.	To obtain a well risen and thoroughly cooked batter.

Biscuits

Biscuits may be made by any of the methods of cake making, but they differ from cakes in:

1. *Consistency of mixture*. This is usually very stiff so little or no liquid is used.

2. *Aeration*. The texture is required crisp so little or no raising agent is used.

3. *Shape and size*. After kneading, the mixture is rolled and cut, or piped into required shape.

4. *Baking temperature*. They are cooked very slowly, so that water is driven off, leaving the biscuits crisp and dry.

Aims in biscuit making

1. *A short crisp texture.* This can be obtained by using a soft flour, or a mixture of cornflour and wheat flour, by slow baking, and by storing in an airtight tin.

2. *Regular shape.* Roll or cut carefully, and have mixture very stiff.

3. *A good colour.* They should be very pale brown. This is obtained by very slow baking.

4. *A pleasant flavour.* Use good quality ingredients in the correct proportions.

Methods of making (see cake making)

1. By melted fat method, e.g. ginger nuts, parkin biscuits, brandy snaps and flapjacks.

2. By rubbing-in method, e.g. shortbread, oatmeal, cheese and coconut biscuits.

3. By creaming method, e.g. Shrewsbury and Easter biscuits, and some shortbread.

4. By the whisking method, e.g. sponge fingers and sponge drops.

Scones

Types

1. Oven scones may be plain, sweet (with fruit, sugar or syrup) or savoury (with cheese). They may be made with flour or a mixture of flour and oatmeal.

2. Girdle scones may be made with a similar mixture.

3. Drop scones may be made from a thick egg batter, and are cooked on a hot girdle or hotplate.

All scone mixtures are plain, i.e. they contain only a small proportion of fat and sugar (see cake making). Except for the batter scones, the method of making is the rubbing-in method. The raising agent may be:

(*a*) Baking powder or

(*b*) Bicarbonate of soda and cream of tartar or

(*c*) Bicarbonate of soda and sour milk.

The mixture should be light and soft in texture, and cooked at a high temperature (200–230°C, Mark 6–8) so that the gases expand quickly and the dough sets quickly. They do not burn easily as they contain little fat or sugar, and for the same reason, they get dry quickly after cooking and should be eaten the same day.

The old slogan for scones was: 'Very cold making, very hot baking.'

Yeast Mixtures

Yeast mixtures are doughs of flour, salt, sugar and a liquid, which are caused to rise by the action of yeast. Rich yeast mixtures may also contain fat, eggs, extra sugar and fruit. The liquid is usually water, milk or a mixture of both.

Ingredients used in cooking with yeast

1. *Flour:* Use a 'hard' or 'strong' flour, i.e. one with a relatively high gluten content. This makes an elastic dough when mixed with water and kneaded. Use plain flour, as no chemical raising agent is needed. If wholemeal flour is used, more liquid will be required as the bran absorbs water.

2. *Salt:* provides flavour and also helps to make a firm gluten framework.

3. *Yeast:* consists of masses of living organisms. These can be mixed with a starchy material and then either dried sufficiently to be compressed into cakes (compressed yeast) or more thoroughly dried (dried yeast) when it will keep wholesome for several months. The dried yeast must be soaked in tepid water before use. Compressed yeast looks like putty; if fresh it should be fawn in colour, crumble easily, have a pleasant characteristic smell, and mix easily with sugar to form a thin liquid. It will keep fresh for about a week if wrapped and stored in the refrigerator, or if kept in a basin of cold water.

4. *Sugar:* provides food for the yeast so that it can grow and begin its work in the dough. The yeast ferments the sugar with the production of carbon dioxide.

5. *Liquids:* Water is needed to help to form the elastic framework of the gluten, to dissolve sugar and salt in the mixture, and to enable the yeast to work. Milk may be used instead of water. This improves the flavour of the dough and increases its food value.

6. *Fat:* is sometimes added to enrich doughs and to improve their keeping qualities. Butter, lard or margarine may be used.

7. *Eggs:* are also sometimes added to enrich the dough.

Aims in yeast cookery

1. *Good appearance.* Loaves, rolls and buns should be regular in shape with an evenly browned outside. This is achieved by skill in shaping and care in baking.

2. *Even rising.* This depends on correct treatment of the yeast, good kneading and careful cooking.

3. *Open and springy texture.* This can be obtained by allowing the yeast to work sufficiently but not to 'overprove', and by placing the dough in a hot oven.

4. *Good flavour* depends on the correct proportion of good quality ingredients. Variety can be obtained by using wholemeal or germ meal flour, or by mixing white flour with rye flour.

General rules for cooking with yeast

1. Use good quality PLAIN flour (preferably 'strong', i.e. one with a high gluten content).

2. Remember great heat kills yeast and cold slows down its activity.

3. Use the correct amount of yeast: 15 g for up to 500 g flour; 25 g for between 500 g and 1½ kg flour; and 50 g for between 1½ kg and 3½ kg flour. Too little will not raise the dough and too much gives a strong flavour.

4. Mix to a soft dough. Too stiff a dough is difficult to knead and slows down the rising. The first kneading helps to mix the yeast thoroughly in the mixture, and the second distributes the bubbles of gas.

5. Allow enough time for the dough to rise to twice its original size, but do not allow to overstretch and so collapse.

6. Bake in a hot oven (230°C, Mark 8) to kill the yeast, and to expand the gases quickly and evenly.

The yeast may be left to rise in a cool place, even in a refrigerator. The rising process will in this case of course be much slower, and in a cool larder or household refrigerator the dough may safely be left for 10–12 hours or overnight. The advantage of cold rising is that a stronger dough is produced and there is little fear of the yeast overstretching the dough, if it is not put into the oven at exactly the right moment.

Principles of cooking with yeast

1. Yeast consists of a mass of single-celled living organisms which when given food and moisture grow by 'budding'. While growing, yeast produces enzymes which act on sugars to split them up into simpler substances. This action, known as *fermentation*, takes place more quickly in warm conditions. In bread making this occurs as follows:

(*a*) Wheat flour when kept moist and warm produces an enzyme, diastase.

(*b*) This diastase acts on some of the starch in the flour and turns it into a form of sugar, maltose.

(*c*) Yeast produces an enzyme, maltase, which turns this maltose into a simpler sugar glucose.

(*d*) Yeast also produces another enzyme, zymase, which turns glucose into carbon dioxide and alcohol. It is the carbon dioxide thus produced which is of chief importance in bread making. Like all gases the carbon dioxide expands when heated and so causes the dough to rise.

Thus: starch is acted on by diastase and turned to maltose. Maltose is acted on by maltase and turned to glucose. Glucose is acted on by zymase and turned to carbon dioxide and alcohol.

2. The gluten framework formed when the flour and water dough is kneaded is elastic. It stretches as bubbles of carbon dioxide are produced. The time taken for the dough to rise depends on temperature, the stiffness of the dough, and the amount of yeast and sugar present.

3. The heat used in cooking bread has the following effects:

(*a*) The yeast is killed and the enzymes are destroyed.

(*b*) The alcohol evaporates.

(*c*) Bubbles of carbon dioxide, water vapour and air throughout the dough expand and stretch the elastic gluten.

(*d*) The gluten framework coagulates or 'sets'.

(*e*) The starch grains swell, burst and absorb liquid.

(*f*) The starch on the outside is turned to dextrin, and the sugar caramelizes making the brown crust.

(*g*) Water evaporates.

Bread making

How

Why

1. Sieve 500 g flour and 1 teaspoon salt into warm bowl and stand in a warm place.

Sieve to aerate and remove lumps. Add salt to give flavour and give firmness to gluten. Keep warm to help yeast to work.

2. Cream 15 g yeast with 1 teaspoon sugar or a little liquid and add to flour, or rub yeast into the flour.

Yeast produces enzymes and begins to act on sugar.

3. Warm 300 ml liquid and add to flour.

Liquid will make a soft dough.

4. Knead dough until texture is smooth and even and it leaves sides of bowl clean.

To make elastic gluten mixture, and to distribute yeast well.

5. Put dough aside to rise until twice its size.

Time is needed for yeast to grow and to produce carbon dioxide which stretches the gluten.

6. Knead lightly and shape into loaves or rolls.

To distribute the gases evenly.

7. Put to rise again (about 10 minutes) in a warm place.

To allow further fermentation.

8. Bake in hot oven (230°C, Mark 8).

To kill yeast, destroy enzymes, to expand the gas and to evaporate the alcohol.

9. Reduce heat after 10 minutes.

To allow time to set gluten throughout the loaf, to burst the starch grains, to allow the starch to absorb liquid and to dextrinize the outside.

How	Why
10. Test for readiness by tapping on bottom of loaf. It should sound hollow.	Gluten framework is set throughout.
11. Allow to cool out of tin.	To allow moisture to evaporate.

A richer dough for buns and doughnuts, etc. may be made by the same method, but the addition of fat and eggs slows down fermentation. For this reason the proportion of yeast is sometimes increased or a preliminary 'sponging' is done. The yeast is creamed with the sugar and liquid added, and this mixture is added to a little of the flour. When fermentation has begun, it is mixed with the rest of the flour, fat and sugar.

ELEVEN

Pudding Making

A pudding or a sweet usually forms a separate course in a meal, and is eaten after the main protein dish. It may provide useful amounts of energy foods in the form of sugar and stärch, as well as protein, fats, vitamins and mineral salts.

Classification of puddings
1. *Flour mixtures* made by any of the pastry or cake making methods:
   (*a*) Suet mixtures, e.g. spotted dog, Christmas pudding.
   (*b*) Suet pastry puddings, e.g. jam roll, boiled fruit pudding.
   (*c*) Baked pastry puddings, e.g. flans, pies, tarts.
   (*d*) Cake mixture puddings, e.g. canary pudding.
   (*e*) Batters, e.g. pancakes, fritters, fruit in batter.
2. *Milk puddings* made of a cereal cooked in milk with sugar and flavouring added, or just made of milk set with rennet.
   Milk cereal puddings. Usually 35 g cereal to 500 ml milk.
   (*a*) Whole grain, e.g. rice, tapioca.
   (*b*) Small grain, e.g. sago, semolina.
   (*c*) Powdered grain, e.g. cornflour, ground rice, custard powder.
   Milk cereal puddings may be served hot, or made into moulds by increasing the amount of cereal, 50 g to 500 ml milk, and served cold. During cooking the starch grains in the cereal swell, burst and absorb the milk. These puddings may be enriched by the addition of eggs.
   Junkets. These are made by adding rennet and a flavouring to lukewarm milk (at 35°C). Rennet contains rennin from the stomach of a calf which coagulates the milk proteins. Do not overheat or the rennin is destroyed. Keep in a warm place until the junket is set.
3. *Egg puddings* in which egg is the chief ingredient.
   (*a*) Omelettes, in which beaten eggs are cooked in hot butter.

(*b*) Custards, in which eggs are cooked with milk.

(*c*) Soufflés, in which egg yolks are added to a panada (a thick white sauce – see page 138) and the stiffly beaten whites are folded in before cooking.

The egg proteins in all egg puddings coagulate with the heat. Over-cooking leads to 'curdling' and must be avoided.

4. *Fruit puddings* may be made with fresh or dried fruit.

(*a*) Fruit may be served raw, stewed or baked.

(*b*) Fruit may be made into moulds, snows, jellies, fools, etc. Cooking softens the roughage in fruit and sieving removes the coarse fibres, making it easier to eat.

5. *Gelatine puddings*, e.g. jellies, creams, cold soufflés. Gelatine is used in the proportion of 10–20 g to 500 ml of milk, fruit juice or purée, cream, custard or a mixture of these. Gelatine is made from the connective tissue of animals but contains incomplete protein. It is sold in powder or in 'leaf' form. It dissolves in hot water and on cooling it sets to a jelly.

6. *Ice-creams* are usually frozen mixtures of custard and cream or fruit purée. Many flavours and textures may be obtained. The mixture may be frozen in a domestic refrigerator or in a special ice-cream freezer.

TWELVE

Stocks and Soups
Use of stock – Types of soups – General rules for making soups.

Stock is liquid obtained from bones, meat, vegetables or fish by long slow simmering, or more quickly by using a pressure cooker.

Why stock is useful
It gives flavour to dishes such as soups, gravies and réchauffé dishes. Although it contains relatively little food value, it does add minerals, vitamins of B complex and a little protein which would otherwise be wasted.

How to make stock

How	Why
1. Choose a strong deep pan with a well-fitting lid.	Food must be covered with liquid, and very little evaporation should take place.
2. Cut meat into small pieces.	To expose maximum surface area.
Use cooked or uncooked meat, gristle or skin, broken bones, poultry giblets, bacon rinds.	
Avoid including too much fat.	To prevent stock being greasy.
Cut vegetables in large pieces.	To prevent vegetables breaking easily and thus making stock cloudy.
3. Add seasoning.	
4. Cover with water or liquor from cooking vegetables or meat.	

How	Why
5. Bring to boil, remove scum.	To prevent stock being cloudy.
6. Simmer for about 2 hours.	To extract all soluble nutrients.
7. Strain and cool.	Solid ingredients are of no further use.
8. Remove fat from top.	Stock should not be greasy.
9. Keep in a refrigerator or a cool place, and boil for 5 minutes daily.	To prevent stock from going bad.

NOTE. Avoid starchy vegetables as these easily go sour. Avoid very strongly flavoured or very salt liquor (e.g. from salt ham) as this gives too strong a flavour to the stock.

Types of stock
1. Meat or bone stock.
2. Vegetable stock for vegetarian dishes.
3. Fish stock for sauces.
4. A quick and simple substitute for stock is a commercial stock cube dissolved in water, which gives flavour but little nourishment.

Soups

The value of soups
1. They act as appetizers by increasing the flow of saliva and gastric juice.
2. They can supply protein, fat or carbohydrate depending on the ingredients used.
3. They can be used to add a hot dish to an otherwise cold meal.
4. They are useful to the cook who wishes to use up small amounts of left-over foods.

Rules for making a good soup
1. Follow the recipe carefully, using correct amounts of the main ingredients.
2. Use stock in preference to water.
3. Season and taste carefully.
4. Make soup of the correct consistency. A purée or cream soup

should be smooth and free from lumps; a broth should have the meat and vegetables in small pieces.

5. Remove all fat.

6. Serve very hot (or alternatively very cold) with the correct garnish.

Types of soups

1. *Clear meat soups or consommés* (these may contain small pieces of vegetable), e.g. Consommé Julienne.

2. *Broths* which contain small pieces of meat, vegetables and cereals, e.g. Scotch Broth.

3. *Purées* which are vegetable soups, sieved and usually thick owing to the ingredients used, e.g. Lentil Soup.

4. *Cream soups* which are made by blending thin vegetable purée with a white roux, e.g. Cream of Celery Soup.

5. *Thickened meat soups*. These are strained and then thickened with flour or cornflour at the end of cooking, e.g. Oxtail Soup.

1. and 2. *Consommés and Broths*

How	Why
1. Cut meat into small pieces, removing fat and skin.	To expose maximum surface area.
2. Put into pan with cold stock, bring to boil, season.	To extract full flavour from meat.
3. Prepare, wash and cut small pieces of vegetables. Add to soup. For a broth, wash and add rice or pearl barley.	For extra flavour.
4. Simmer gently.	To cook contents.
5. When making consommés, strain off solid particles.	Consommé should be clear.
6. Taste the soup before serving.	Seasoning can be adjusted.
7. Garnish with chopped parsley.	To improve appearance.
8. Serve very hot.	

3. and 4. *Vegetable Soups (Purées and Creams)*

How	Why
1. Prepare vegetables and cut into small pieces.	To enable flavour to be extracted.
2. Sauté vegetables in melted fat.	To develop flavour and improve food value.
3. Add cold stock, bring to boil, add seasoning and taste the soup.	
4. Simmer until vegetables are cooked.	
5. Sieve, put through a vegetable mill or blender.	To give a smooth consistency.
6. *For a Purée:* Thicken, only if necessary, with a little blended cornflour.	
Boil well.	To cook cornflour.
Serve very hot with croutons.	
For a Cream Soup: Blend with a white roux sauce.	To give extra food value and richer texture.

5. *Thickened Meat Soups, e.g. Kidney, Oxtail*

How	Why
1. Prepare meat and vegetables and cut into small, even-sized pieces.	To ensure extraction of flavour and even cooking.
2. Fry until golden brown.	To give colour and flavour.
3. Add stock and seasoning.	
4. Bring to boil, simmer until tender.	To cook ingredients.

How	Why
5. Strain solids from the liquid.	Flavour should be in the liquid.
6. Add blended flour and boil well.	To give a smooth texture.
7. Taste the soup. Serve very hot. Garnish with a few small pieces of meat.	Seasoning can be adjusted.

THIRTEEN

Beverages

Beverages is the name given to all drinks which supply the body with the water necessary to maintain health.

Why we need beverages

1. To supply water necessary to build the body tissues and for carrying out the complex chemical processes of metabolism. (See Chapter 1.)

2. To refresh us, and to quench our thirst which is an indication of the body's need for water.

3. To supply nourishment, e.g.

(*a*) Milk drinks supply animal proteins, fats, minerals and vitamins.

(*b*) Fruit juices if fresh and properly prepared contain vitamin C.

(*c*) Drinks sweetened with sugar, glucose or lactose supply carbohydrates and extra Calories.

4. To act as stimulants, e.g. tea and coffee contain caffeine, and cocoa contains theobromine; these have a mild stimulating effect on the nervous system.

5. To improve the flow of gastric juices, e.g. meat extracts such as Bovril and Oxo, or yeast extracts such as Marmite, stimulate the appetite because of the extractives they contain. Some also supply all the vitamins of B complex.

6. To give an immediate sense of warmth and comfort when the body is cold.

Common beverages

1. *Tea:* is obtained from the leaves of a shrub grown mainly in India, China and Sri Lanka. The leaves are picked, crushed and dried. In this state they are known as green tea. They may then be moistened and allowed to ferment before re-drying. This produces the common black tea. Tea has very little food value, but supplies

caffeine which is a nerve stimulant, tannin which is an astringent and can give a bitter flavour, and the essential oils which give tea its aroma.

2. *Coffee:* is obtained from the fruit of a shrub grown in South America, East Africa and elsewhere. Each fruit contains two seeds or beans. These are removed from the husk, roasted and ground. Coffee contains small amounts of caffeine, more tannin than tea does, and essential oils which give the flavour. Ground coffee exposed to the air soon loses the essential oils, and therefore its flavour. 'Instant coffee' is produced by the dehydration of liquid coffee.

3. *Cocoa:* is obtained from the seeds of a small evergreen tree grown in South America and in West Africa. The seeds (or 'nibs') contain fat which is removed and used as cocoa butter. The rest is ground into a fine powder. Cocoa has more food value than either tea or coffee. It contains fat, starch and small amounts of protein, vitamins and mineral salts, as well as the stimulant theobromine.

4. *Fruit drinks*, e.g. fresh lemon, orange juice. These are chiefly of value for their vitamin C content, and for their refreshing taste. Care must be taken not to boil the juice because this would destroy the vitamin C.

5. *Alcoholic drinks.* These are made by the fermentation of the maltose in malted grains, or the glucose in fruit juices, into carbon dioxide and alcohol. Alcohol has a sedative effect on the central nervous system and this action may seriously affect one's judgment and self control. The amount of alcohol varies with the type of drink.

(*a*) Beers, stouts and ales contain 5–10 per cent of alcohol, and are made from malted barley.

(*b*) Wines such as sherry, claret and port contain 10–20 per cent alcohol and are made from grape juice.

(*c*) Spirits, e.g. gin, whisky, brandy, contain about 40 per cent alcohol and are made from liquids fermented and then distilled to increase their alcoholic content.

(*d*) Liqueurs are sweetened and flavoured spirits.

6. *Mineral waters.* Some are naturally produced from springs in the earth and are bottled at source, e.g. Vichy water. They contain dissolved mineral salts and carbon dioxide. Others are synthetic products made by charging sweetened and flavoured water with carbon dioxide under pressure, thus making it fizzy.

To make household beverages

1. *Tea*

How	Why
(a) Warm the pot and put in ½–1 teaspoon of tea for each person, i.e. to each 250 ml water.	Amount used depends upon personal taste.
(b) Pour on actually boiling water and allow to stand 2–3 minutes.	To extract caffeine and essential oils.
(c) Serve at once.	To avoid extracting tannin.
(d) Add milk, sugar or lemon as desired.	

2. *Coffee*

How	Why
(a) Warm pot or jug and put in 1 tablespoonful of ground coffee for each 250 ml of water.	
(b) Pour on boiling water and stir well.	To mix well.
(c) Leave to infuse in a warm place for 8 minutes.	To extract flavour and caffeine.
(d) Strain through a fine wire strainer.	To remove grounds.
(e) Serve black or with hot milk, or cream and sugar as desired.	

3. *Cocoa*

How	Why
(*a*) Mix cocoa (1 rounded teaspoon for each 250 ml) with a little cold liquid, and sugar to taste.	To blend starchy powder to a smooth paste.
(*b*) Boil remaining milk and/or water and pour on to blended cocoa.	To make a smooth mixture.
(*c*) Return to pan and boil.	To cook starch and to develop flavour.

4. *Fruit drinks (orange and lemon)*

How	Why
(*a*) Peel or grate rind of fruit thinly and place in pan with sugar and water.	Flavour is mostly in zest, and pith is often bitter.
(*b*) Boil gently for 5 minutes.	To extract the flavour.
(*c*) Strain and allow to cool.	To remove peel.
(*d*) Squeeze juice from fruit and add to cold liquid.	Heat destroys vitamin C.

FOURTEEN

Sauces, Gravies, Seasonings, Flavourings, Accompaniments and Garnishes

Sauces are prepared liquids used in the preparation of dishes or served as accompaniments. They are often thickened and may be sweet or savoury.

Why sauces are used
1. To add flavour to otherwise insipid foods, e.g. onion sauce with mutton.
2. To add colour to colourless foods, e.g. tomato sauce with white fish.
3. To improve the food value of a dish, e.g. mayonnaise with a salad.
4. To counteract the richness of certain foods, e.g. apple sauce with pork.
5. To moisten dry foods, e.g. custard sauce with steamed puddings.

Classification of sauces
1. Those made with a roux of fat and flour, e.g. white sauce, thick brown gravy.
2. Those thickened by blending and cooking starchy cereals, e.g. cornflour, arrowroot, custard powder.
3. Those thickened with egg: (*a*) *Cooked*, e.g. egg custard, or (*b*) *Uncooked*, e.g. mayonnaise.
4. Miscellaneous sauces, e.g. fruit sauce, mint sauce, bread sauce.

1. *Roux sauces may be:*
(*a*) white (*b*) brown (*c*) with added egg. The quantities of ingredients used depend upon the required thickness.

(*a*) *White roux sauces*
(i) A pouring sauce for serving cold, or for moistening foods: Use 15 g flour, 15 g fat and 300 ml liquid (usually milk).

(ii) A coating sauce for covering or coating food: Use 30 g flour, 30 g fat and 300 ml liquid.

(iii) A binding sauce or panada used for binding food, e.g. fish cakes: Use 60 g flour, 60 g fat and 300 ml liquid.

To make white roux sauce

How	Why
1. Melt fat in pan, add flour, stir and cook gently until it 'honeycombs'. Stir continuously with a wooden spoon. (This is a white roux.) Do not brown.	Starch grains in flour burst on heating and absorb fat, giving glossy appearance to finished sauce. Browning spoils appearance of a white sauce.
2. Remove from heat, and add liquid gradually, stirring all the time.	Sauce should be smooth and free from lumps.
3. Return to heat and bring to boil, stirring all the time.	Starch grains swell and absorb liquid thus thickening sauce.
4. Boil for 4–5 minutes.	To cook starch thoroughly and so to avoid 'raw' taste.
5. Add seasoning and flavourings, e.g. anchovy, grated cheese, chopped parsley.	

(*b*) *Brown roux sauce*

Use 15 g flour, 15 g fat and 300 ml vegetable or meat stock.

To make brown roux sauce

How	Why
1. Heat the dripping or lard in a thick pan, add flour. Stir and cook until mixture is golden brown in colour. (This is the brown roux.)	Starch grains swell and absorb fat. Some starch is turned to dextrin, giving the required brown colour.

How	Why
2. Add cold stock slowly, stirring well. As temperature of the roux is above 100°C add liquid with care.	To make sauce smooth and glossy. Steam is produced very quickly.
3. Bring to boil and cook for 5 minutes.	To develop flavour and to cook thoroughly.
4. Season, serve hot as gravy, or use for meat dishes.	

NOTE. As dextrin is soluble, this sauce is less likely than the white sauce to become lumpy when the liquid is added.

(c) *Roux sauces with an egg added* (Hollandaise, etc.). Add beaten eggs or yolks to a white roux sauce after making. Heat gently but do NOT boil after egg is added, or egg protein will coagulate and give a curdled appearance.

2. *Blended sauces* (thickened with cereal, e.g. cornflour, arrow-root).

(a) A pouring sauce: Use 15 g ground cereal to 300 ml liquid.

(b) A coating sauce: Use 25 g ground cereal to 300 ml liquid.

How	Why
1. Blend powder with a little cold liquid.	To keep grains apart.
2. Boil rest of liquid and pour over blended powder stirring well.	To swell and burst the starch grains.
3. Return to heat, and boil for 4 to 5 minutes stirring all the time.	To cook starch thoroughly to avoid raw taste.
4. Add seasoning, or sugar and flavouring.	

NOTE. If an egg is used, add to cooked sauce after cooling slightly. Reheat gently but do not boil, to avoid curdling.

3. *Sauces thickened with eggs*
  (*a*) *Cooked, e.g. egg custard.* Use 1 egg to 175 ml milk.

How	Why
1. Beat egg slightly.	To mix yolk and white but not enough to incorporate air.
2. Heat milk to approx. blood temperature and pour on to beaten egg, stirring well.	
3. Heat gently, preferably in a double pan or over a low heat, stirring well until sauce thickens slightly. Do not boil.	Gentle heating causes even coagulation of egg proteins and even thickening of sauce. Boiling causes curdling.

  (*b*) *Uncooked, e.g. mayonnaise.* Use 1 egg yolk to about 175 ml oil.

How	Why
1. Mix yolk with seasoning.	
2. Add oil drop by drop stirring all the time, as it thickens.	The egg proteins hold an emulsion of oil in the yolk.
3. Slowly add vinegar or lemon juice.	To flavour and to make to a coating consistency.

4. *Miscellaneous sauces*
  (*a*) *Apple sauce* served with roast pork, consists of apple purée slightly sweetened. It counteracts the richness of the meat.
  (*b*) *Bread sauce* served with roast chicken consists of white bread or crumbs simmered with onion in seasoned milk until of a creamy consistency. It gives flavour and food value to the chicken.
  (*c*) *Mint sauce* served with roast lamb consists of finely chopped mint in sweetened vinegar. It adds flavour to the meat.
  (*d*) *Horseradish sauce* served with roast beef consists of finely grated horseradish in cream or evaporated milk. It adds flavour and pungency to the meat.

(*e*) *Jam, or marmalade sauce* served with steamed or baked puddings is made by boiling jam (or marmalade) with sugar and water until a syrupy consistency is obtained. It moistens and flavours the puddings, and may be thickened with arrowroot if desired.

Gravies

Gravies are served with roast meats, and should be well flavoured with extractives from the meat itself. It is usual to serve an unthickened gravy with roast beef, pork, chicken and duck, and a thick gravy with lamb, veal, goose and turkey.

(*a*) *Thickened gravy*

How	Why
1. Remove meat from roasting tin.	
Pour off nearly all fat, but retain the meat juices.	Gravy must not be too greasy. To give a good flavour.
2. Add 1 rounded tablespoonful flour, mix well and cook over heat for 2–3 minutes.	To thicken. Starch grains swell, burst, and absorb fat, and some starch is dextrinized.
3. Add 500 ml stock or vegetable water, stir until boiling. Boil 5 minutes. Season and strain.	To cook starch thoroughly and to develop flavour.

(*b*) *Thin gravy*

How	Why
1. Pour off as much fat as possible.	To avoid greasiness.
2. To the sediment add 1 teaspoonful of flour, and 500 ml stock or vegetable water.	To give a smooth consistency.
3. Boil for 2 minutes.	To cook starch thoroughly.

Seasonings, Flavourings, Accompaniments and Garnishes

Seasonings are added to foods to bring out the natural flavours of the foods, to make insipid foods appetizing and to stimulate the flow of gastric juices.

1. *Salt:* obtained from brine.

(a) It is a source of sodium and chlorine in the diet.

(b) It helps to improve the natural flavours of foods.

(c) It strengthens the gluten in flour mixtures.

(d) It acts as a preservative for many foods.

Table salt usually has rice flour or sodium phosphate added, to keep the salt dry, as salt itself is very hygroscopic, i.e. it absorbs water from the air. Iodized salt is useful in districts where the soil and water are deficient in iodine.

2. *Pepper* is obtained from a tropical plant, the fruit of which is dried and ground. If the fruit is unripe, black pepper is obtained; if ripe, white pepper. Pepper contains an essential oil which stimulates the flow of digestive juices.

Cayenne pepper is made from ground dried chillies. It has a very strong flavour, and is used in curries, etc.

Paprika pepper is made from ground dried capsicum. It has a mild flavour and is used chiefly for its decorative red colour.

3. *Vinegar* is made by the action of bacteria on the alcohol of wine, cider or malt liquors. The alcohol is 'soured' or turned to acetic acid.

(a) It is used to flavour fish, salads, etc.

(b) It acts as a preservative, as micro-organisms cannot flourish in acid solutions.

(c) It is used in cooking for sousing fish, marinating meat, etc.

4. *Lemons* supply both juice and the outer rind or 'zest'. Fresh lemon juice is an important source of vitamin C and when possible should be so used that the juice will not be heated.

5. *Spices* are now used to give extra flavour and variety to foods. In earlier times they were used to disguise disagreeable flavours.

(a) *Ginger* is the underground stem of a tropical plant. It can be dried, preserved in syrup, or ground and used in cakes and puddings.

(b) *Cinnamon* is the bark from the shoots of a tropical shrub. It is dried and used either in stick form or when ground to a powder.

(*c*) *Cloves* are the flower buds of a tropical tree. The buds are dried and used whole in puddings, etc.

(*d*) *Mixed spice* is a mixture of ground ginger, cinnamon and cloves.

(*e*) *Capers* are the flower buds of a tropical shrub. They are pickled in salt and vinegar, and used in sauce.

(*f*) *Celery seed* is the seed of the celery plant. It is ground and used in soups and stews.

(*g*) *Caraway* is the seed of a plant. These seeds are dried and used to flavour cakes and buns.

(*h*) *Nutmeg* is the kernel of the fruit of a tropical tree. These kernels are dried and grated on milk puddings, etc.

(*i*) *Mace* is the outside husk of the fruit of the nutmeg tree. It is dried and powdered and used in stews and soups.

(*j*) *Mustard* is made by grinding the seed of the mustard plant. Dried, it is used in pickles and chutneys; ground and mixed with water or vinegar it is used as a condiment.

(*k*) *Chillies* are the dried pods of a species of capsicum or red pepper. They have a strong flavour and are used sparingly.

(*l*) *Curry powder or paste* is a mixture of ginger, pepper, turmeric, chillies, nutmeg, etc., and is used in stews and curries.

(*m*) *Allspice* comes from the ground, dried berries of the Jamaica pepper tree or pimento, and is used to flavour savoury dishes.

(*n*) *Vanilla* is the seed pod of a tropical plant. The dried pod may be kept in a container of sugar to which it will impart a delicate flavour. An extract of vanilla in alcohol is used as a flavouring essence in cakes, puddings, etc.

6. *Herbs* are derived from plants containing pungent and fragrant essential oils. They are best used fresh and finely chopped. They may however be dried and powdered. Herbs supply flavour, and when fresh also a little vitamin C. The most common herbs in use in England are mint, parsley, thyme, sage, marjoram, fennel, rosemary and chives. Bay leaves may be used fresh or dried and are usually added whole and removed before serving the food.

Garlic is the bulb of an onion-like plant. It has a very strong flavour, and should be used very sparingly.

A bouquet garni is a bunch of herbs, e.g. bay leaf, thyme, parsley, etc. tied in a small muslin bag with peppercorns. It is used to flavour soups and stews. It is cooked in the liquid and always removed before serving.

7. *Flavouring essences.* These may be the essential oils of the plant

dissolved in alcohol; more usually nowadays they are artificial chemical substances. Most are very volatile and are therefore better added after cooking. Examples are vanilla, lemon, almond, peppermint essences.

8. *Colourings* also may be natural products (e.g. cochineal and saffron) or artificial dyes.

9. *Garnishes* are decorations added to dishes just before serving to improve both appearance and flavour. They are usually edible, e.g. lemon slices with fish, chopped parsley with soup, parsley sprigs with any fried food, crystallized cherries with cold sweets.

10. *Stuffings or forcemeat* are usually mixtures of breadcrumbs with some fat and herbs, e.g. sage and onion, lemon, parsley and thyme, chestnut. They add flavour and nourishment to meat, fish and poultry.

11. *Accompaniments* are served with dishes to add food value or to improve the colour, flavour and texture.

Dish	Accompaniment
Thin Soup.	Shredded or diced vegetables, noodles or macaroni.
Thick Soup.	Fried or toasted bread croutons.
Fish: grilled or fried.	Lemon slices, parsley butter, parsley, tomato or tartare sauce.
Fish: boiled, steamed or baked.	Anchovy, cheese or parsley sauce, colourful vegetables.
Meat:	Gravy or a sauce. Green or root vegetables, or a green salad. Potatoes.
Grilled or fried.	Mushrooms, tomatoes, watercress, parsley butter.
Roast Beef.	Horseradish sauce, Yorkshire pudding.
Roast Lamb.	Mint sauce.

Dish	Accompaniment
Roast Pork or Duck.	Apple sauce and sage and onion stuffing.
Roast Chicken.	Bread sauce, bacon rolls. Chipolata sausages, stuffing.
Roast Mutton.	Onion sauce, red currant jelly.
Steamed Puddings and Pies.	Sweet or custard sauce.
Salads.	Salad dressing or mayonnaise.
Vegetables (e.g. cauliflower).	White coating sauce. Melted butter.

FIFTEEN

Home Preservation of Fruit and Vegetables
Causes of decay – Principles underlying preservation – Methods used in the home.

Preservation is undertaken to prevent decay, and to keep the food as near to the fresh state as possible.

Causes of decay

1. *Enzymes* in the food itself, i.e. chemical substances which act as catalysts and speed up chemical changes which otherwise would proceed very slowly. An example of these changes is the browning of some fruit when cut and exposed to air. Enzymes work quickly in warm conditions but more slowly in cold. They are destroyed by heat.

2. *Micro-organisms,* i.e. minute forms of life which get into food or on to its surface, and which need warmth, moisture and air for their growth. Micro-organisms are of three classes:

(*a*) Moulds which grow on the surface of food, spoiling its appearance and taste.

(*b*) Yeasts which grow in the presence of sugar.

(*c*) Bacteria which attack and break down proteins, fats and carbohydrates.

Principles of preservation

1. To destroy by heat any enzymes or micro-organisms in the food.

2. To prevent the enzymes or micro-organisms causing deterioration:

(*a*) by removing air or water, *or*

(*b*) by reducing the temperature, *or*

(*c*) by the use of a strong concentration of sugar, salt or vinegar. *or*

(*d*) by the use of chemical preserving agents.

3. To prevent the further access of micro-organisms to the food by careful storage (e.g. in tins or tightly sealed jars).

Why food should be preserved

1. Economy: To prevent waste and to save surplus food for later use.

2. Convenience: Bottled and canned foods are a help in making quickly prepared meals.

Methods of home preservation and why they work

1. *Drying or dehydration:* The removal of water prevents the action of enzymes and micro-organisms, e.g. dried apple rings, herbs.

2. *Cold storage:* This prevents decay as the organisms are inactive below a certain temperature, e.g. in the storage of food for short periods in a domestic refrigerator, or for long periods in a deep-freeze cabinet.

3. *Jam and jelly making:* The cooking destroys the enzymes and micro-organisms, and the 60 per cent sugar solution prevents the growth of any micro-organisms which may enter from the air.

4. *Bottling and canning:* The heating destroys the micro-organisms and enzymes initially present, and the air-tight seal prevents the entry of any other micro-organisms from the air.

5. *Pickling:* The heating destroys the enzymes and micro-organisms initially present, and the vinegar being acid prevents the growth of any which may enter the bottle or jar later.

6. *Salting:* The strong salt concentration removes water by osmosis from the food and also from the micro-organisms, thus preventing their growth.

7. *Addition of chemical preservatives:* e.g. Campden tablets which contain sulphur. These destroy the micro-organisms and enzymes in the first place, and the weak solution remains sterile in a stoppered vessel.

1. *DRYING*, e.g. dried apple rings.

How   Why

1. Wash, peel and core apples, To remove dirt.
 cut into $\frac{1}{2}$ cm slices.   To expose maximum surface area.

How	Why
2. Put into salt solution for 10 minutes. (1 level tablespoon salt to 1 litre water.)	Colour is preserved, water from fruit is drawn out by osmosis.
3. Rinse well and dry.	To remove taste of salt.
4. Thread on strings and hang in a warm place at 60°C.	To allow remaining water to evaporate, thus stopping enzyme action.
5. When they have the texture of chamois leather, store in a covered jar in a cool, dry, dark place.	They are dehydrated enough to prevent the growth of micro-organisms.
6. Before use, soak in water for 24 hours.	To replace the water removed by drying.

2. *FREEZING*, using a home freezing cabinet.
Suitable for preserving meat, poultry, vegetables and fruits.

How	Why
1. *Preparation*	
(*a*) Prepare meat by cutting into suitable sized joints.	
(*b*) Prepare poultry by plucking, drawing and trussing.	
(*c*) Prepare vegetables by blanching and boiling for short time, draining and cooling.	Blanching destroys enzymes in vegetables.
(*d*) Prepare fruit by covering with sugar or syrup.	To improve flavour.
2. *Packing*	
Pack food into moisture-vapour-proof bags or boxes, with as little air in them as possible.	To prevent evaporation of water and drying of food, and to prevent strong smelling foods tainting others.

How	Why
3. *Freezing* Set freezer to —30°C to —35°C.	Rapid freezing ensures only small crystals of ice which do not damage cell structure.
4. *Storage* Store at —16°C.	The lower the temperature the less deterioration during storing.
5. *Use* After removing, allow to thaw but use quickly. Do *not* re-freeze.	So that organisms of decay having become active on the thawing will have no time to cause deterioration.

3. *JAM MAKING*

Qualities of good jam

(a) Distinct fruity taste. This depends on the quality of the fruit.

(b) Clear and bright of colour. This depends on the acid content.

(c) Well set but not too stiff. This depends on the pectin (see below) and the acid content and on the length of time of boiling.

(d) Good keeping properties. This depends on the sugar content which should be about 60 per cent.

Principles of jam making

1. Fruit contains a gum-like substance called PECTIN, and also a certain amount of acid. When sugar, pectin and acid are present in the correct proportions and the jam is boiled it will set (or 'jell') on cooling.

2. Some fruits (apples, blackcurrants, gooseberries, plums and all citrus) are rich in pectin and will easily make jams, jellies or marmalades. Other fruits (cherries, melons, strawberries) are poor in pectin. When these are made into jam, extra acid in the form of lemon juice may be needed to help the jam set; or they can be mixed with a fruit rich in pectin; or commercial pectin may be used.

3. The fruit is simmered in the first stage of jam-making to soften it, to release the pectin and to destroy the enzymes and micro-organisms present.

4. Sugar is then added and should be in the proportion of about 6 parts of sugar by weight to 10 parts of the finished jam. Micro-organisms cannot grow in this concentration of sugar.

5. The jam is boiled quickly to make it set, and to 'invert' some of the cane sugar and thus to inhibit crystallization.

6. The jam is put in jars and covered to discourage the entry of micro-organisms from the air. It is then stored in a cool, dry place.

To make jam

How	Why
1. Choose fruit which is just ripe and still firm.	At this stage it contains the greatest amount of pectin.
2. Weigh, wash and place (with water if necessary) in large preserving pan.	A large pan gives the greatest area for evaporation.
3. Simmer fruit slowly.	To soften the fruit and to release the pectin.
4. Add acid if necessary	To help to release the pectin.
5. Add sugar and stir with a wooden spoon, 1 kg sugar to 1 kg fruit is the average. Fruits rich in pectin will take more sugar.	
6. Allow to boil rapidly.	To invert some of the cane sugar and to reach setting point.
7. Stir occasionally	To prevent sticking and burning.
8. Test for a set after about 10 minutes with a little on a cold plate, or boil until temperature reaches 105°C.	Too long boiling at this stage spoils the colour of jam.

How	Why
9. Pour into hot clean jars.	Hot jars crack less easily.
10. Cover with wax paper and cellophane covers.	To discourage entry of micro-organisms.
11. Store in a cool, dark, dry place.	To discourage the growth of micro-organisms.

4. BOTTLING

Bottling is a process in which fruit is packed into clean bottles or jars; they are then sterilized, and sealed with special tops to prevent the entry of air. Canning (which is not normally carried out in the home) depends on the same principles but the cans are sealed before sterilization.

Principles of bottling

1. Fruit is heated slowly in the jars, either in the oven or in a pan of water, so that the enzymes and micro-organisms are destroyed but the fruit remains whole.

2. While still hot the jars are sealed. The partial vacuum formed under the lid as the contents cool keeps the seal firm, and prevents the entry of micro-organisms from the air.

3. The jars are stored in a cool, dark, dry place, thus providing conditions in which micro-organisms do not flourish.

To bottle fruit

How	Why
1. Choose fruit firm and just ripe.	Such fruit will keep its shape and is less likely to decay than over-ripe fruit.
2. Prepare and wash as for stewing.	
3. Prepare a syrup of about 250 g sugar to 500 ml water. Boil and cool.	Syrup sweetens fruit and improves the flavour.
4. Choose jars which are sound, clean and with well-fitting lids.	To ensure an airtight seal.

How

Why

5. EITHER

Pack fruit tightly into wet jars and fill to the top with syrup.

Fruit shrinks in cooking and will rise in the jars unless tightly packed.

Place in a pan on an asbestos mat, with cold water up to the necks of the jars. Place the lids lightly on the jars and SLOWLY raise the temperature to 90°C (simmering point) in about ½ hour. Keep soft fruits at this temperature for 2 minutes, hard fruits for 10 minutes. Screw or clip down immediately.

Heat destroys the enzymes and micro-organisms and fruit should remain whole if heating is slow.

To prevent entry of air and to create a partial vacuum as the jars cool.

OR

Pack fruit into jars but do not add the syrup. Place jars in a slow oven (150°C, Mark 2) and heat slowly. As the fruit shrinks, fill up the jars with fruit from a spare one. Soft fruit takes ½ hour, hard fruit longer. When cooked, remove one jar at a time; fill with boiling syrup and place on the lids and screw tops at once.

6. Cool for 24 hours and then test for a seal by removing screw or clip and lifting jar by the lid.

To make sure that no air can enter.

7. If seal is firm, store in a cool dry place.

Bottling of vegetables

This should not be attempted without a pressure cooker. Unlike fruit, vegetables are non-acid and the organisms of decay can flourish in them at higher temperatures than in fruit. By using a pressure cooker with a medium weight, a temperature of 115·3°C can be reached, which is sufficient to preserve vegetables safely. However, great care should be taken as faulty processing can result in food poisoning. Pressure cooker manufacturers provide detailed instruction for vegetable bottling and these should be followed very carefully.

5. *PICKLING AND CHUTNEY MAKING*

In these preserves, vinegar is an important ingredient as it provides the acid which inhibits the development of micro-organisms. Spices add flavour.

Pickling (onions, red cabbage, cucumbers, etc.)

How

Why

How	Why
1. Prepare vegetables as for cooking. Cut if necessary.	For convenience in packing.
2. Soak for 24 hours in brine (100 g salt to 500 ml water).	To reduce water content of vegetables by osmosis.
3. Rinse and drain.	To remove excess salt.
4. Pack into jars, leaving 1 cm at top.	To allow vinegar to cover vegetables completely.
5. Heat 1 litre vinegar with 25 g pickling spice and allow to cool.	
6. Pour vinegar into jars.	Vinegar enters vegetables, replacing their water content by doing so.
7. Cover tightly with non-metal covers.	To prevent evaporation. To prevent acid attacking the cover.

Chutney making (apple, gooseberry, tomato, marrow, etc.)

How	Why
1. Cut or mince ingredients into small pieces.	To make it easier to pulp.
2. Cook in a little water until soft.	
3. Add vinegar, spices and sugar and cook gently until thick.	To reduce the water content and to blend the flavours.
4. Bottle in hot jars.	To prevent cracking of jars.
5. Cover as for pickles.	

6. *SALTING*

In this process water passes from the food by osmosis and is replaced by the salt solution, e.g.:

(*a*) Salting of meat or fish by placing between layers of dry salt, or in a solution of brine.

(*b*) Salting of runner beans in dry salt.

Salting of runner beans

How	Why
1. Slice beans as for cooking.	To expose a large area to the salt.
2. Arrange a layer of salt on the bottom of an earthenware or glass container. Place on this a 2 cm layer of beans.	Salt prevents the action of enzymes and micro-organisms.
3. Repeat with alternate layers of dry salt and beans, finishing with a layer of salt.	
4. Fill the jar the next day with further layers as beans sink.	Water extracted from the beans dissolves some of the salt.
5. Cover and store in a cool, dark, dry place.	To prevent loss of colour.

To use salted beans, soak for 1 to 2 hours, drain and cook in water without salt.

7. *CHEMICAL PRESERVING*

Campden tablets containing sulphur can be used for preserving certain fruits such as apples and plums by following the instructions supplied with the tablets.

How

Why

1. Prepare fruit as for stewing. For convenience in packing.

2. Pack into preserving jars.

3. Crush Campden tablets and dissolve in cold water. Pour on to fruit. Sulphur dioxide is produced. Micro-organisms and enzymes are destroyed.

4. Cover and store in a cool dry place.

To use fruit preserved in this way, put the fruit into a saucepan without a lid and boil gently until all the sulphur dioxide is driven off. Sweeten to taste.

SIXTEEN

Kitchen Hygiene
Food spoilage – Food contamination – Larders,
refrigerators and freezers – How to choose and use them.

Correct hygiene of the kitchen is of great importance because upon it depends the health of the family. Food must be correctly handled and stored, in order to:

1. Avoid spoilage in appearance or taste, whereby the food becomes unpalatable.

2. Avoid contamination, whereby it becomes harmful to eat.

1. *How food can be spoilt*

(*a*) By becoming too dry, e.g. green vegetables wilt, fruit and root vegetables shrivel, bread becomes stale.

(*b*) By becoming too wet, e.g. sugar becomes lumpy; crisp foods, such as biscuits, become soft.

(*c*) By the action of enzymes in the foods themselves, e.g. fruit rots and changes colour.

(*d*) By the action of micro-organisms from the air, e.g. moulds on the surface of bread and jam, yeasts in fermenting fruit juices and bottled fruit, bacteria in the souring of milk, putrefaction of fish and meat. (See also Chapter 15.)

(*e*) By animal or insect pests, e.g. weevils in cereals.

How to prevent food spoilage

(*a*) By storing food whether raw or cooked under the most suitable conditions (see also under individual foods).

  (i) Meat, milk, butter and cheese in covered containers in a
      cool place.
 (ii) Vegetables in a well ventilated rack in a cool, dark place;
      salad vegetables in a covered container, or a polythene
      bag in a refrigerator.
(iii) Bread in a ventilated bin; cakes and biscuits in separate
      tins.

(iv) Dry stores in glass, earthenware or plastic containers with lids.

(v) Tinned goods in a dry, cool place.

(*b*) By planning the larder properly, and by the intelligent use of a refrigerator. If there is a refrigerator and a dry store cupboard there is no real need for a larder.

2. *How food can become contaminated*

Sometimes tainted food may be quite indistinguishable from wholesome food in taste and appearance, but it has become contaminated in some way so that if eaten it causes symptoms of food poisoning, e.g. stomach pains, vomiting, diarrhoea. This 'contaminated' food must not be confused with food which has been spoilt by poor storage.

Food poisoning may be caused by:

(*a*) Certain poisonous foods, e.g. berries or fungi. (Some people are allergic to some foods, i.e. they react to ordinary foods, e.g. strawberries, shell-fish, eggs, which do not affect other people.)

(*b*) Certain metallic substances present in the food, e.g. arsenic from fruit sprays, zinc from galvanized vessels used for cooking.

(*c*) The presence of harmful bacteria in the food, e.g. (i) *Salmonella bacteria* from the intestines of man and animals. (ii) *Staphylococci* which are present in the nose and throat, and in septic cuts, boils, etc. These form a toxin which contaminates food. (iii) Miscellaneous bacteria causing similar symptoms. (iv) *Bacilli* causing botulism which is rare but very dangerous. The spores are resistant to heat. The bacilli produce toxins which have a serious effect on the central nervous system.

Foods most likely to cause food poisoning

1. Meat and made-up meat dishes, e.g. sausage meat, brawn, meat pies.

2. Milk and milk dishes, e.g. synthetic cream, ice-cream.

3. Soups, gravies, stews.

4. Eggs (particularly ducks' eggs).

5. Fish.

The following conditions encourage the growth of food-poisoning bacteria: warmth, moisture and air. They multiply very rapidly; time is therefore an important factor.

Ways in which to prevent contamination of food

1. *By paying attention to personal hygiene, especially by*

(a) Frequent hand washing, particularly after use of lavatory.

(b) Covering all cuts and sores with clean dressings.

(c) Not coughing or sneezing near food.

(d) Wearing clean overalls and hair coverings.

(e) Not handling food unnecessarily.

(f) Not working with food when one has a cold or a stomach upset.

These points should apply to all who handle food.

2. *By cleanliness of kitchen premises and equipment*

(a) All working surfaces must be clean and in good repair.

(b) Kitchen must be kept free from pests, e.g. mice, flies, cockroaches.

(c) Pets must not be allowed near human food.

(d) Washing-up must be done in really hot water and all utensils should be rinsed well before being left to dry in a rack.

(e) If drying cloths are used they must be spotlessly clean.

(f) All dish cloths, teatowels, mops, etc. must be washed regularly.

3. *By care over the disposal of waste*

(a) All decayable rubbish must be kept in well covered containers which are frequently emptied and washed out.

(b) Dustbins must be tightly covered, kept away from the windows of the kitchen, and regularly emptied, cleaned and disinfected.

4. *By care over the storage of foods*

General rule: 'Keep food clean, cool and covered.'

It is best to use a refrigerator or a ventilated larder.

(a) *Meat.* Keep in a refrigerator, or hang in a meat safe, or keep under wire gauze in a cool place. Rub with salt and vinegar if it is necessary to keep it for long before cooking. Do not partly cook meat one day and finish cooking later. This encourages the growth of bacteria. When reheating meat, heat it thoroughly, do not make it just warm.

(b) *Milk.* Keep in a refrigerator or in coolest possible place. Never leave milk standing in the sun, as ultra violet light destroys the vitamin C. In hot weather milk may be kept in a bottle or jug standing in a vessel of cold water, covered with muslin, with the ends dipping into the cold water. If no refrigerator is available, scald milk in very hot weather if intending to keep it overnight.

(c) *Left-overs.* Keep covered in a cool place, and use as soon as possible. Scald soups, gravies, stews, etc. before serving them again.

(d) It is difficult to keep fish fresh; it should be put in a covered container in a refrigerator to keep it overnight in warm weather.

Use and care of a larder: planning a larder

How	Why
1. Position should be near kitchen on outside wall, if possible on north or north-east side.	For convenience. To keep as cool as possible.
2. Must have ventilation, if possible by window on outside wall.	To keep air fresh.
3. Window should be covered with perforated metal sheet.	To keep out flies and other pests when window is open.
4. Should have well placed electric lighting.	For convenience at night.
5. Walls and ceiling should be smooth, in good repair, and light in colour.	For easy cleaning. For good illumination.
6. Floors should be smooth and cool, made of materials such as clay or thermoplastic tiles.	For easy cleaning.
7. Shelving should be shallow, easily reached and covered with a washable surface.	For convenience in storage, and for easy cleaning.

How	Why
8. A meat safe and a vegetable rack are useful in the larder.	For hygienic storage.
9. All foods must be stored on clean plates or in clean containers. Use left-over foods as soon as possible.	
10. Larder must be kept scrupulously clean. Each week remove contents, wipe shelves and walls, clean windows and floor. Daily, keep tidy.	

Refrigerators

The low temperature of a refrigerator enables perishable food to be kept for several days, as it reduces the activity of microorganisms and enzymes which cause deterioration. Usually the temperature is kept at between 5°C and 8°C (40°F and 45°F) in the main part; in the ice box it is about −9°C (15°F). The low temperature is produced by a device in which liquid is made to evaporate, taking heat from its surroundings as it does so. Afterwards the gas thus produced is cooled and condensed for use again.

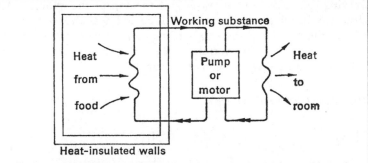

Fig. 14. The refrigerator. When the refrigerating liquid (or working substance) evaporates to form gas in the freezing unit, heat is taken from the food in the refrigerator. The gas is compressed by a motor or pump, the working liquid is reformed and heat is given off to the outside air. The refrigerator should therefore not be fitted in an enclosed space.

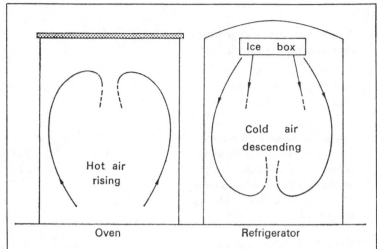

Fig. 15. *Circulation of air in an oven and a refrigerator. Convection currents are created when air is heated or cooled locally. Heating air makes it less dense: cooling makes it denser. The cooler, denser air flows downwards and pushes up the warmer air.*

A refrigerator may be run by electricity, gas or paraffin. It consists of a double walled cabinet, usually of pressed steel finished with vitreous enamel, with the space between the layers filled with heat-insulating material, such as glass fibre. The freezing unit (ice box) is usually at the top of the cabinet. Air circulates inside the refrigerator. It is cooled near the ice box and falls to the bottom of the cabinet, taking heat from the contents. The warmer air at the bottom is pushed up again by the heavy cold air coming down (convection currents).

Use and care of a refrigerator

How	Why
1. As the temperature is controlled by a thermostat, set the control at a number which will keep the temperature of the cabinet at 5°C.	For economy of fuel.

How	Why
2. Pack foods carefully but not tightly together.	To allow free circulation of air.
3. Pack foods in correct position as suggested by the manufacturer's chart.	To make best use of low temperatures.
4. Always cover foods (polythene bags are useful).	Foods will become dry and flavours mixed if left uncovered.
5. Always allow food to cool before putting in refrigerator.	Hot food slightly raises the temperature of the interior. This is wasteful of fuel.
6. The refrigerator ice box may be used for temporary storage of frozen foods.	Frozen food will deteriorate slowly if allowed to thaw.
7. Clean and de-frost regularly, unless it automatically defrosts itself.	Deposit of frost forms round freezing unit. This will reduce efficiency.
8. Avoid opening door more than necessary.	This wastes fuel.

Defrosting and cleaning

1. Turn the thermostat to the index mark specified in the maker's instructions.

2. Remove all food and leave door open.

3. Place drip tray under the freezing unit.

4. Remove ice trays, empty and refill with fresh water.

5. Remove shelves, wash in warm water and dry well.

6. When all frost has melted, clean inside cabinet with a weak solution of sodium bicarbonate or of borax (about 1 tablespoon of bicarbonate or 1 teaspoon borax to 4 litres of water). Do not use soap. Dry thoroughly.

7. Wipe the outside with a clean, damp cloth.

8. Polish any chromium fittings with a soft, dry cloth.

9. Turn thermostat control to required number, replace food and close door.

10. When leaving the house with the power turned off (as when

going on holiday), switch off the refrigerator and leave the door of the refrigerator open to ensure free circulation of air. This will prevent mould forming.

Deep freezers

These are used for preserving foods for longer periods and at lower temperatures than in the freezing compartment of a refrigerator. They work on the same scientific principles as refrigerators – i.e. evaporation and compression of a liquid refrigerant. During evaporation heat is absorbed from the food in the freezer, and during compression the heat given up passes into the outside surroundings.

How to choose and to use a freezer

How	Why
1. Choose between (a) Chest type with top opening lid. (b) Upright type with front opening door. (c) Combined freezer refrigerator with two separate doors.	To consider price, easy storage, easy cleaning and amount of floor space available.
2. Size – depends on number in family and amount it is used.	More space needed if used for storing garden produce, bulk bought meat etc.
3. Position must be cool, dry and well ventilated – e.g. pantry, corridor or large kitchen.	Running costs are less if set in a cool place.
4. Use only fresh food in perfect condition. Handle food with great attention to hygiene, and always follow the makers' instructions.	Freezing inhibits bacterial action but does not destroy bacteria.
5. Avoid unnecessary opening of door or lid.	To avoid formation of frost.
6. Defrost occasionally following makers' instructions.	Necessary for efficient and economical running.

SEVENTEEN

Kitchen Planning
Planning the layout of the kitchen – Cookers: types and choice – Oven temperatures – Sinks – Working surfaces – Small equipment – Weighing and measuring of ingredients.

The kitchen should be an efficient and pleasant workshop for the housewife. A good kitchen should be:

1. Conveniently placed in the house (not like the Victorian basement).

2. Planned to save time and effort.

3. Easy to keep clean and free from steam and grease.

4. Planned for the safety of the occupants, with special precautions where children are in the family.

When planning a kitchen the following points should be considered:

How

Why

Aspect
The kitchen is probably best facing east, with, if possible, an open view from the window.

To give morning sunshine and to prevent a feeling of isolation.

Position in house
Near dining area and near back door.

For general convenience and to avoid walking long distances.

Size
This depends on the way in which it is used. If it is merely a workroom, about 8 sq m is a reasonable area. If it is used for meals also, about 12 sq m is better.

Too large a room wastes time and energy, and too small a room is cramping to work in and difficult to keep tidy.

How	Why

Shape
A rectangular shape is probably better than a square.

For a given area this gives longer wall space where equipment can be placed.

Position of doors
Doors should not be on opposite walls nor placed so that they foul each other when opened.

To avoid draughts and accidents.

Position of the main equipment
Cooker and sink should be close together with working surfaces near both, and if possible near window. Storage for food and utensils should be near sink and cooker. There should be a flat surface near the door.

To avoid unnecessary steps.

To give good light.

To receive parcels and food packets from outside.

Lighting
Windows should be large and not too high. Artificial lighting must be well placed to give adequate light over all main working positions.

To ease the work and to make accidents less likely.

Ventilation
This must be thoroughly efficient. It is usually by doors and windows but probably the best method of ventilation is by an electric extractor fan.

To get rid of steam and food smells and to ensure a supply of fresh air.

Space heating
This must be adequate. Solid fuel cookers or water heaters also warm the kitchen. Oil, electric or gas radiators may be used. Avoid portable heaters and trailing flexes.

Comfort of the worker is essential although kitchens vary greatly in the amount of heating required.
These are dangerous, as they may cause falls.

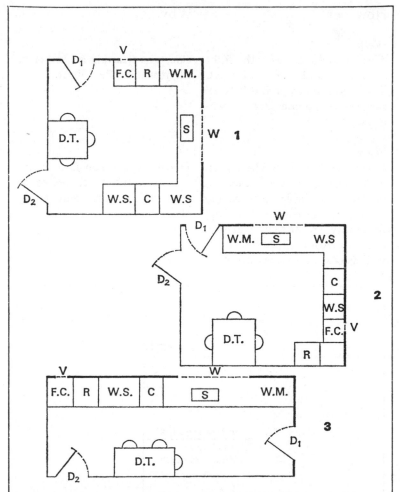

Fig. 16. The diagram illustrates the arrangement of equipment in three kitchens of different shapes but of equal area. 1. Square kitchen with equipment on three walls. 2. Oblong kitchen with equipment on two walls. 3. Long, narrow kitchen with equipment on one wall. D₁ is outside door, D₂ is door to rest of house. W. window, V. ventilator, F.C. food cupboard, R. refrigerator, C. cooker, D.T. dining table, S. sink, W.S. working surface with cupboards and shelves, W.M. work-surface with washing appliances underneath. Thick lines show the outside walls.

How	Why
Walls	
These should be smooth, light in colour and easily cleaned. There are many suitable wall surfaces to choose from nowadays.	Constant cleaning is necessary. Light walls reflect light.
Floors	
Floor coverings should be chosen from the wide range of modern products available, considering such points as ease of cleaning, durability, resilience, warmth, freedom from slipperiness, as well as cost and appearance.	Floors require constant cleaning; they should therefore be resistant to dirt and easily cleaned.

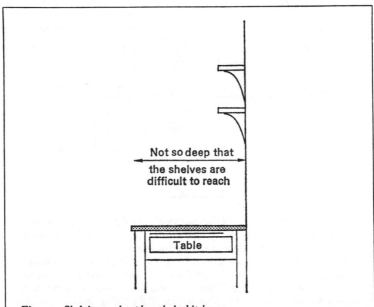

Fig. 17. Shelving and cupboards in kitchens.
Arrange so that they are easy to reach, not too high, not too far from the worker, and conveniently spaced.

How

Why

Position of storage areas
Cooking pots, tools and utensils should be near the cooker and working surfaces (table, etc.). Cleaning materials near sink.

To save unnecessary work in carrying.

Food: Fresh vegetables near sink.

Dry goods near working surface.

Perishable goods in a refrigerator, or a ventilated larder.

Position of laundry equipment
Clothes boiler, washing machine, etc. should be near the sink. Spin dryer, etc. can be under the working surface and near power plugs.

Safety precautions
Arrange good lighting. Store everything needed within easy reach. Avoid traffic through kitchen when possible. Provide adequate supervision of children and old people.

The most common accidents in the kitchen are burns, scalds, cuts and falls.

Provide adequate first aid box.

Colour scheme
This is entirely a personal matter but the kitchen decor should provide a light, cheerful background.

The kitchen should provide the best working environment possible.

Cookers

The cooker is the most important piece of equipment in the kitchen. The heat for cooking is obtained usually from:

(a) Solid fuel
or (b) Coal gas, Calor gas, natural gas, etc.
or (c) Electricity
or (d) Paraffin
or (e) Fuel oil.

A cooker consists of an oven for baking, together with a hot plate for boiling, frying, etc., and with usually some arrangement for grilling. It is made of sheet steel with a vitreous enamel finish which is easy to keep clean. About 70 per cent of the heat used in family cooking is supplied by the hot plate, which is usually about 91 cm above floor level. The width and depth of the cooker vary with its size. A wide oven is easier to use than a deep one.

1. *Solid fuel cookers*
A solid fuel cooker usually has a fire box with one or two ovens at the side, and a hot plate over both fire and oven. The hot gases from the fire circulate round the oven which is a steel box. The semi-insulated cooker is constructed so as to reduce heat loss, and usually has a cover to place over the hot plate when the cooker is not in use. The rate of burning is controlled by dampers; there is often a back boiler to supply hot water. The heat-storage cooker is more heavily insulated with an automatically controlled hot plate and oven. The oven usually is kept at about 205°C–230°C. A second, cooler, oven is often provided too.

2. *Gas cookers*
The oven is a double walled box of sheet steel with a heat-insulating layer between the walls. It has a well-fitting door; burners are fixed at the bottom either at the back or the sides. There is a flue to remove the products of combustion. All modern cookers have controls with lettered or numbered dials operating the thermostatic devices. The hot plate is placed either alongside or above the oven, and contains a set of gas rings and a grill. The grill is sometimes fixed at eye level.

3. *Electric cookers*

These resemble gas cookers in design, but the oven is heated from elements sometimes fitted in the side walls, and sometimes under the floor of the oven. The hot plate is usually fitted above the oven and has several boiling rings either of the solid type, or of the quick heating radiant types. The grill element is usually a coil of high resistance wire fitted under a solid plate, heat being radiated from the red-hot wire down on to the food placed below.

4. *Oil cookers*

These range from simple paraffin cookers to modern oil-fired insulated cookers. The rate of burning is controlled by knobs which regulate the oil flow. Since oil is highly inflammable great care should be taken when using this type of cooker. The oil in the cooker should never be replenished while it is alight, and spare cans of paraffin or oil must never be left near a lighted cooker.

How to choose a cooker

How	Why
Points to consider:	
1. *Fuel available*	
Whether gas, electricity, coke, anthracite or other smokeless fuel.	Usually all available in towns; gas is often not available in country except in portable gas containers.
2. *Use to which it will be put*	
If required for space and water heating as well as for cooking.	Only a solid fuel cooker will do all three.
3. *Cost*	
Thing to consider here is not only the initial cost but also the running costs of the cooker.	Solid fuel cookers are often more expensive to buy but cheaper to run. Gas and electricity are about equal on both counts if used intelligently.

How	Why
4. *Size* Great variety available. Choose one large enough for the needs of the family but not too big for the kitchen.	A solid fuel cooker really needs a large kitchen.
5. *Efficiency* Gas is quick heating and easily regulated.	Instant heat is available from burning gas, taps regulate flow easily.
With electricity the equipment is usually slower to reach working temperature and reacts slowly to any adjustment.	Time must be allowed for the hot plates to heat and to cool. Radiant burners are quicker.
Solid fuel has everything always at working temperature but, like oil, is slow to regulate and more skill is required in using it.	
6. *Labour involved in use* Gas and electricity involve very little work, solid fuel and oil need more.	Work is necessary to refuel, to clear ashes, etc.
7. *Cleanliness in use* Electricity is the cleanest.	No fuel is burnt in an electric stove.
	The gaseous products of combustion from a gas stove have to be disposed of.
	Solid fuel produces dust, ashes and soot, various gases and perhaps smoke if a smokeless fuel is not used.
	Oil produces carbon deposits and sometimes fumes.

How	Why
8. *Ease of cleaning* Most stoves are coated with vitreous enamel. The smooth surfaces of electric and solid fuel cookers are usually more easily cleaned than those of gas burners. Steel surfaces should be kept lightly oiled.	To prevent rust when not in use.
9. *Safety* Check that gas taps are turned off and out of reach of small children.	Coal gas is poisonous and forms an explosive mixture with air.
Check that an electric cooker is 'earthed'. Turn off before cleaning.	To avoid risk of shock.
Handles of pans, pans with hot fat, etc. on all cookers should be so disposed that accidents cannot occur.	There is risk of burns and scalds if pans are carelessly placed.
10. *Appearance* Most modern cookers are neat and of pleasing design. Choose a colour and style to fit the general colour scheme.	With so wide a choice colour and design are purely a personal matter.

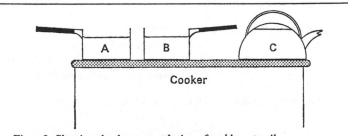

Fig. 18. Showing the dangerous placing of cooking utensils.

(*A*) *The handle should not protrude like this.*

(*B*) *The handle, if placed over the actual cooker, may become dangerously hot.*

(*C*) *Kettle is dangerously near the edge and the escaping steam may cause scalds.*

How to use cookers

To get good results, to avoid waste of heat and to minimize risk of accidents, the cooker must be used intelligently. The following points must be considered.

How

Why

1. *Choice of cooking pan*

For all solid hot plates a flat bottomed heavy pan is necessary. On electric radiant plates and on gas, a lighter pan may be used.

A good thermal contact is necessary between hot plate and pan for efficient conduction of heat.

2. *Use of hot plate*

Allow gas (or oil) flames to touch bottom of pan, but not to come round the sides.

To minimize loss of heat.

On electric plates, have pan large enough to cover the hot plate and switch off before the end of cooking.

To minimize loss of heat.

To utilize residual heat in the hot plate.

On a solid fuel cooker keep hot plate covered when not in use.

To avoid loss of heat.

Keep surfaces of hot plates and pans clean.

Grease and dirt are poor heat conductors. Their presence causes a thin film of air between the metal surfaces.

Use a pressure cooker when possible.

To economize on fuel.

3. *Use of oven*

Always cook as much food as possible at one time, and place in the oven intelligently.

To make best use of oven heat.

How	Why
Use a baking sheet under dishes when possible.	Easier to handle, and this often avoids accidents.
Switch off electricity before end of cooking.	Oven stays hot and the available heat can be then utilized.

4. *Cleaning*

How	Why
Wipe out electric and gas ovens while still warm.	Grease and dirt are easier to remove while warm.
Wipe up spilt or splashed food from all cookers immediately.	Easier to remove.
For a periodic clean, take out removable parts and clean by washing with hot water and a detergent. (Electric elements must not be made wet.)	
Vitreous enamel stoves should be washed, and stubborn marks removed with soap and steel wool with care to avoid scratching.	A coarse abrasive will scratch the surface.
Metal parts must be dried thoroughly by heating the stove after cleaning it.	To prevent rust forming.

Oven temperatures

Every modern cooker is fitted with a thermostat, i.e. a device for keeping the oven at a chosen temperature. This temperature may be selected by turning a dial which shows either the required temperature, or letters or figures which correspond.

	Temperature in degrees		
State of oven	*Fahrenheit*	*Celsius*	*Dial number*
Cool	200–250	100–130	$\frac{1}{4}$–$\frac{1}{2}$
Slow	275–300	140–150	1–2
Moderate	325–350	170–180	3–4
Fairly hot	375–400	190–200	5–6
Hot	425–450	220–230	7–8
Very hot	475–500	240–260	9

Some cookers are fitted with an automatic device which will switch the heat on and off at any given time. These are very useful to the busy person.

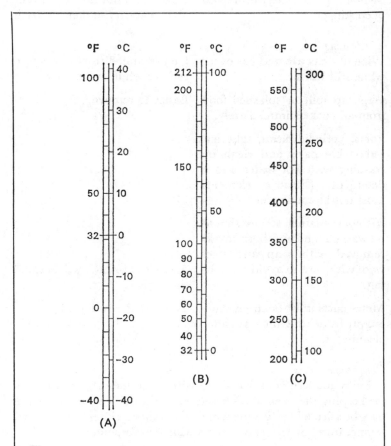

Fig. 19.

(A) The range of temperatures reached in kitchens, larders, refrigerators and deep-freeze cabinets.

(B) Temperatures between the boiling and freezing points of water.

(C) The range of temperatures reached during cooking by such methods as baking, grilling and frying.

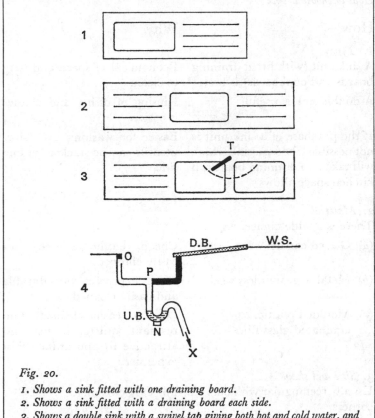

Fig. 20.

1. Shows a sink fitted with one draining board.

2. Shows a sink fitted with a draining board each side.

3. Shows a double sink with a swivel tap giving both hot and cold water, and with one draining board.

4. Shows a section through a sink.

D.B. is a sloping draining board, O. is the overflow running into the pipe below the plug hole P. U.B. is the U bend containing a water seal. N. is the nut which may be removed for cleaning. W.S. is the working surface. X. leads to the outside drain.

Sinks

Much of the work done in the kitchen is at the sink, which should be supplied with both hot and cold water and a waste pipe for emptying. The sink should be at a convenient height from the ground.

How to choose a sink

How	Why
1. *Type*	
A sink unit (with fitted draining boards and cupboards) is best.	Economical of space and easy to clean.
A double sink is useful.	Rinsing of dishes and clothes is easier.
If the purchase of a sink unit is not possible, choose a sink which will take two draining boards, if kitchen space allows.	Easier for washing up. Dirty utensils can be stacked on one side.
2. *Material* There is a wide choice, e.g.	
(*a*) Glazed earthenware.	Cheap, easily cleaned, but easily chipped.
(*b*) Metal, e.g. stainless steel.	More expensive but durable and easily cleaned.
(*c*) Moulded plastic, e.g. laminated glass fibre.	Durable, easily cleaned, stain resistant, quieter in use and attractive in appearance, but expensive.
3. *Size and shape* Usually rectangular with curved corners.	For easy cleaning.
Deep enough and wide enough.	To avoid splashing surroundings and to take a washing bowl.
Of a suitable height.	For comfortable working.
4. *Position and surroundings* Best position is:	
(*a*) On outside wall.	For ease of plumbing.
(*b*) Near window.	For good light.
(*c*) Near cooker and work-surface.	To save carrying pans.
Surroundings must be smooth, e.g. tiles, enamel paint.	For easy cleaning.

How	Why
It is convenient to have cupboards fitted near the sink.	For storing cleaning and laundry materials.

5. *Sink fitments*

How	Why
(a) Taps should be of stainless material.	To save cleaning.
Taps should be at least 30 cm from bottom of sink.	For ease of filling buckets, etc.
(b) Draining boards, of hardwood or stainless steel, should slope towards sink.	To allow water to drain off.
(c) Overflow outlet, a stopper for the waste pipe, and a grating over the waste outlet should be fitted.	To avoid flooding, blockages, etc.

How to use and to clean the sink

How	Why
1. Use a sink-tidy of enamel or polythene.	To collect rubbish and to avoid blocking wastepipe.
2. Keep very clean, using warm water, soap and a recommended cleaner.	
3. Flush with tap water after cleaning.	To leave clean water in U-trap.
4. Disinfect regularly and use a bleach if required.	
Occasionally pour hot soda water into U-trap.	To remove grease.
5. If U-trap gets blocked, use a sink plunger.	To remove the trouble by varying the pressure in pipe.
or	
Unscrew nut under trap (with a bucket underneath) and clean pipe with a brush.	To remove blockage.

Working Surfaces in the Kitchen

One or more flat surfaces are necessary in every kitchen for food preparation. The surface may be a table top, the top of a low floor-cupboard, a let-down flap from the wall or a continuation of the sink unit. It should be hard, smooth, stain resistant, quiet to work on, resistant to cutting edges, pleasant to look at and of reasonable cost. It should be arranged at a convenient height for the user – a very important point to minimize fatigue.

How to choose and to use working surfaces

How

Why

1. *Position*
It must be near the sink and cooker, must be well lit, of a reasonably large size, and of convenient height, not too wide.

For the convenience of the housewife. Too small a surface cramps the work.
To eliminate stretching and stooping.

2. *Material*
Choose between:

(*a*) Wood.

Cheap, durable, quiet, but needs scrubbing.

(*b*) Stainless steel.

Smooth, easily cleaned but noisy in use and expensive.

(*c*) Vitreous enamel.

Smooth, easily cleaned but noisy in use and chips easily.

(*d*) Laminated plastic.

Smooth, easily cleaned, stain resistant and pleasant in appearance, but can be scratched, and blistered by heat.

How

Why

3. *Use*

(*a*) Do not chop or cut directly on them but use a hard chopping board.

To maintain working surfaces in good condition.

(*b*) Do not place very hot pans or irons on them. Use a stand.

(*c*) Remove all flour, scraps, etc. before washing; wash all surfaces with warm soapy water (scrub the wood the way of the grain); rinse and dry well. Remove stains with steel wool and soap, or use a mild bleach.

Small Equipment for the Kitchen

When buying small equipment, choose:

1. The best quality you can afford. It will last longer.

2. Equipment easy to clean and to keep in repair.

3. Implements which are comfortable to use and of the right size for the work in hand.

4. Those with a good design and with a good finish, pleasant to look at.

The quantity bought depends upon the amount of cooking to be done.

EQUIPMENT	CHOICE	CARE
1. *Wooden articles* Chopping board Rolling pin Wooden spoons Pastry board (unless working surface can be used)	Hard woods, e.g. teak, oak, give better wear	Scrub the way of the grain, rinse well. Dry in air. Bleach occasionally

EQUIPMENT	CHOICE	CARE
2. Cloths Oven cloth Floor cloth Tea towels Dish cloth Hand towels A roll of muslin for use as meat cloths, etc.	Choose absorbent material which can be easily washed and boiled	Wash in hot water. Rinse, boil and dry in open air
3. Cutlery Vegetable knife Cook's knife and fork Palette knife Potato peeler Kitchen scissors Ladle Fish slice Spoons (3 sizes)	Stainless steel is easy to keep clean but for sharp cutting edges carbon steel is better For spoons nickel plate is satisfactory	Sharpen knives frequently. Wash in hot soapy water, do not soak unless handles are riveted. Remove stains with steel wool
4. Earthenware, glass, ovenware or china Mixing bowl Pudding basins Pie dishes Casseroles Jelly moulds Plates	Choose ware with a good protective glaze. Heat resisting glassware is useful	Soak to remove remains of starchy mixtures. Wash and dry well
5. Brushes Pastry brush Vegetable brush Nail brush Small scrubbing brush Pan scourers (may be nylon)	Nylon bristles are easier to keep clean and stiffer than natural bristles	Wash, rinse in cold water and hang to dry
6. Tinware (or aluminium) Roasting tin Baking sheets Cake tins Sandwich tins Bun trays Cooling tray Graters Pastry cutters Whisk	Choose heavy gauge tinned sheet steel or aluminium. See that tinned steel has no sharp edges	Wipe while still hot, wash in hot soapy water. Dry well and store in a dry place

EQUIPMENT	CHOICE	CARE
Tin-opener, corkscrew, bottle-opener	Choose one which does not call for great skill or physical effort on the part of the user	Keep absolutely clean

7. *Pots and pans*

Saucepans (at least 3) with lids Kettle Shallow frying pan Deep fryer with lid Double saucepan Steamer (to fit large saucepan)	1. Aluminium, which is hard-wearing and easy to clean 2. Enamel, which is hard wearing and easy to clean but chips easily 3. Stainless steel, which is excellent but heavy and expensive	Soak immediately after use; burnt pans must be soaked in salt water. Wash in hot soapy water and use steel wool or nylon scourer to remove stains. Rinse and dry well

NOTE. Pans must be flat-bottomed for use on solid hot plates, must have heat-resisting handles, well-fitting lids with knobs and be well balanced with wide bases.

8. *Scales, knife sharpener, mincing machine, etc.* are also needed.

9. *Plastic ware* (bakelite, polythene, etc.)

Storage jars and salt and pepper containers Lemon squeezer Flour dredger Liquid measure Colander Strainer Set of measuring spoons Washing-up bowl Covered bin for rubbish	There is a wide choice in this ware. It is light, pleasant in appearance, easy to clean and not easily broken	Avoid using them near a source of heat as some may soften and melt. Wash in warm water and dry well

10. Other utensils (although not really essential) help by saving time. Such things include rotary whisks, food mixers and blenders, egg slicers and pressure cookers. If more elaborate cooking is done such things as soufflé dishes, forcing bags, dariole moulds and a sugar thermometer are also helpful.

11. Fire blanket, fire extinguishers, first-aid box.

The Weighing and Measuring of Ingredients

For good results in cookery, ingredients should be weighed or, if no scales are available, measured. Many cooks of long experience are capable of estimating with considerable accuracy the amounts of ingredients required, but estimating by guesswork is not a practice to be recommended to the student.

How to weigh

Use reliable scales. There are two main types of scales for domestic use:

1. *Balance scales with weights:* These are the more accurate. The scale pan should move freely before you begin. The correct weight is obtained when the food on the scale pan just balances the weights on the other so that both sides are level.

2. *Spring scales:* The indicator needle should be pointing to zero before you begin. The correct weight is obtained when the indicator needle is pointing to the required weight on the dial.

How to measure

In America all ingredients are measured by the Standard Cup (8 fluid ounces). The British Standard Cup of 10 fluid ounces has been replaced by a range of cup measures, and there is also a new range of standard spoon sizes. These are:

Cup

measures: 50 ml 75 ml 100 ml 150 ml 300 ml

Spoon

measures: 1·25 ml 2·5 ml 5 ml 10 ml 15 ml 20 ml

Measuring jugs are practical as they provide a range of measures marked out on a useful piece of kitchen equipment. Usually they are graduated in decilitres but some have smaller graduations. Many are marked to give approximate measure of dry ingredients such as sugar and flour, though it must be remembered that these are not always very accurate.

Measuring liquids: Spoon or cup measures should be filled until they are almost overflowing. Measuring jugs should be placed on a flat surface and the reading taken at eye level to ensure as much accuracy as possible.

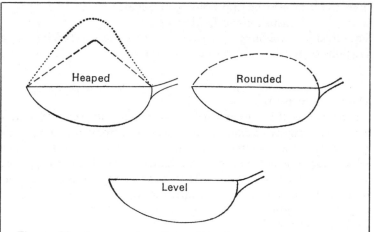

Fig. 21. How to measure ingredients with a spoon.

A heaped spoonful is obtained by having as much as possible above the rim. A rounded spoonful is obtained by having as much above the rim as there is in the bowl. A level spoonful is obtained by levelling off the top with a knife.

Measuring dry ingredients: The terms 'level', 'rounded' and 'heaped' spoonfuls are often used. The diagram shows what is meant by these. Many people use ordinary household spoons for measuring but since these are not in standard sizes, the results may be unsatisfactory. Obviously, level spoonfuls are more accurate measures than rounded or heaped spoonfuls. If using a measuring jug, this should be shaken gently so that the dry ingredient will level off, before the reading is taken.

Some handy measures

With dry ingredients, the number of spoonfuls which make up a given weight will vary according to the density of the ingredient being measured. The following is a rough guide:

1 tablespoon (15 ml) water, milk or other liquid	= 20 g
1 tablespoon jam, honey, syrup or treacle	= 25 g
1 rounded tablespoon flour, cornflour, cocoa or custard powder	= 20 g
1 rounded tablespoon sugar	= 25 g
1 rounded tablespoon rice, dried fruit	= 30 g

The 50 ml measuring cup holds 50 g sugar.
The 75 ml measuring cup holds 50 g flour.
Packaged fats weighing 250 g (or 8 oz.) can be divided into 25 g
portions by marking off into ten divisions.

Conversion tables

There may well be times when conversions between metric and
Imperial weights cannot be avoided. You may be using non-
metric equipment or recipe books, or you may be in a country
which does not use metric units. Exact conversions usually give
very awkward figures and it is simpler to use rounded equivalents. It is unlikely that the slight differences that rounding off
makes to weights and volumes would make any appreciable
difference to a recipe.

The following conversion tables may prove helpful. Exact
equivalents are shown in the brackets.

Weight			
	25 g	1 oz.	(0·88 oz.)
	50 g	2 oz.	(1·76 oz.)
	75 g	3 oz.	(2·64 oz.)
	100 g	4 oz.	(3·53 oz.)
	150 g	6 oz.	(5·29 oz.)
	250 g	8 oz.	(8·88 oz.)
	300 g	10 oz.	(10·64 oz.)
	375 g	12 oz.	(13·23 oz.)
	500 g	1 lb.	(17·64 oz.)
	1,000 g (1 kg)	2 lb.	(2·20 lb.)

Volume			
	25 ml	1 fl. oz.	(0·88 fl. oz.)
	50 ml	2 fl. oz.	(1·76 fl. oz.)
	125 ml	5 fl. oz.	(4·39 fl. oz.)
	175 ml	$\frac{1}{3}$ pt.	(6·15 fl. oz.)
	250 ml	$\frac{1}{2}$ pt.	(8·78 fl. oz.)
	375 ml	$\frac{3}{4}$ pt.	(13·16 fl. oz.)
	500 ml	1 pt.	(17·55 fl. oz.)
	1,000 ml (1 litre)	2 pt.	(1·76 pt.)

Length			
	$\frac{1}{2}$ cm	$\frac{1}{4}$ in.	(0·20 in.)
	1 cm	$\frac{1}{2}$ in.	(0·40 in.)

Length	2·5 cm	1 in. (0·98 in.)
	5 cm	2 in. (1·97 in.)
	10 cm	4 in. (3·94 in.)
	15 cm	6 in. (5·90 in.)
	18 cm	7 in. (7·08 in.)
	20 cm	8 in. (7·87 in.)

NB. Metric cake tins are perfectly suitable for non-metric recipes. That is, the mixture for a 15 cm tin will fit a 6 in. tin, that for an 18 cm tin will fit a 7 in. tin, and vice versa.

Temperature

A very wide range of temperatures can be found in many kitchens, with refrigerators and freezers very cold and ovens very hot. Figure 19 on page 176 shows temperature scales in both Fahrenheit and Celsius (Centigrade).

To convert Fahrenheit to Celsius: subtract 32 and multiply by $\frac{5}{9}$.

To convert Celsius to Fahrenheit: multiply by $\frac{9}{5}$ and add 32.

Oven temperatures: Many gas ovens have numbered settings, which are equivalent to the temperature readings in degrees usually shown on electric ovens. A table of oven temperatures is shown on page 175.

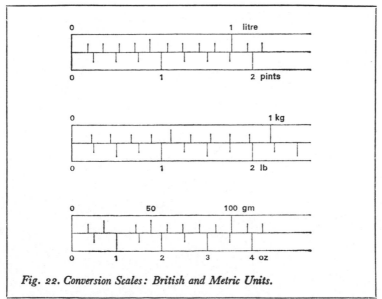

Fig. 22. Conversion Scales: British and Metric Units.

Index